CW00816207

A SHORT
FACILITATING RISK
MANAGEMENT

A Short Guide to Facilitating Risk Management

Engaging People to Identify, Own and Manage Risk

Penny Pullan and
Ruth Murray-Webster

Illustrations by
Vanessa Randle

Routledge
Taylor & Francis Group

LONDON AND NEW YORK

First published 2011 by Gower Publishing

Published 2016 by Routledge
2 Park Square, Milton Park, Abingdon, Oxon OX14 4RN
711 Third Avenue, New York, NY 10017, USA

Routledge is an imprint of the Taylor & Francis Group, an informa business

British Library Cataloguing in Publication Data
Pullan, Penny.
A short guide to facilitating risk management : engaging people to identify, own and manage risk. – (Short guides to business risk series)
1. Risk management. 2. Risk managers. 3. Industrial management – Employee participation.
I. Title II. Series III. Murray-Webster, Ruth.
658.1'55-dc22

Library of Congress Cataloging-in-Publication Data
Pullan, Penny.
A short guide to facilitating risk management : engaging people to identify, own and manage risk / Penny Pullan and Ruth Murray-Webster.
p. cm. – (Short guides to business risk)
Includes bibliographical references and index.
ISBN 978-1-4094-0730-0 (hbk. : alk. paper) – ISBN 978-1-4094-0731-7 (ebook : alk. paper)
1. Risk management. I. Murray-Webster, Ruth. II. Title.
HD61.P85 2011
658.15'5–dc22

2010054245

Reprinted 2014

ISBN 9781409407300 (pbk)

Contents

List of Figures and Tables

About the Authors

PENNY PULLAN

The majority of Penny Pullan's work is with people in multinational organisations who are grappling with tricky projects and programmes of change. Tricky usually means a combination of:

- risky, with uncertain outcomes;

- working with virtual team members dispersed around the globe;

- complex and often ambiguous requirements; and

- complex and often culturally diverse mix of stakeholders, who need to be interested, engaged and involved.

With this context, Penny brings order and clarity, providing support and tools to cut through the problems and to emerge successful, delivering benefits at the same time as developing the individuals involved. Her facilitation skills are fundamental to her work, especially in risk management.

Penny is an entertaining and engaging public speaker, dramatically illustrating how you can apply the tips and tricks described in this book to powerful effect in your own organisation.

Clients of Penny's company, Making Projects Work Ltd, include Novo Nordisk, Abbott Laboratories, AstraZeneca, Johnson & Johnson, Quintiles, the UK NHS and other government departments, ESI, the National Grid, several leading UK Universities and international charities, banks, insurance companies, telecoms and IT providers.

info@makingprojectswork.co.uk
www.makingprojectswork.co.uk
+44 (0) 1509 821691

RUTH MURRAY-WEBSTER

Ruth Murray-Webster is an organisational change consultant, Managing Partner of Lucidus Consulting Ltd, and a Visiting Fellow at Cranfield School of Management.

Her professional interests and experience centre on the competences required for individuals to manage change and the capabilities that organisations need to improve and advance. In recent years Ruth has worked extensively with a variety of large organisations helping them to achieve tangible business benefit from their investment in risk management.

Ruth holds a Master of Business Administration degree from Henley Management College where she carried out research into the effect of cultural differences on business success within international joint ventures. She is currently studying for a Doctorate at Cranfield School of Management, researching planned change to work routines from the perspective of the workers whose job is being changed.

ruth@lucidusconsulting.com
www.lucidusconsulting.com
www.ruth.lucidusblog.com
+44 (0) 1484 818560

FACILITATING RISK MANAGEMENT

WWW.FACILITATINGRISK.COM

How useful would you find risk management support, tailored specifically to what you need right now to succeed in your own organisation?

We have written this book to provide very practical guidance that can be applied immediately. However, for those who would like more support to facilitate risk management so that people identify, own and manage risks, we have two special programmes.

These programmes are for people who have knowledge of risk management processes, tools and practices (as described in Chapter 2), but who struggle to get people in their organisation enthused and committed enough to make risk management work and deliver real value.

OPTION 1: TWO-DAY RISK FACILITATION SKILLS WORKSHOP

Do you need to run risk workshops and other group meetings or sessions where risk is the topic? If so, this is the programme for you. We cover both face-to-face and virtual techniques and practise them to build your skills, so you can apply them with confidence back in your organisation.

This workshop focuses on the practical skills of facilitation, applied to making risk management work well. It is a hands-on event with a facilitator per eight participants. We keep this low facilitator to participant ratio so that people will receive specific guidance and feedback on their own issues.

To get you going quickly, we will provide you with some material prior to our workshop using our virtual learning environment. After the workshop, you'll be invited to a teleseminar to share your post-course achievements and challenges. You will be able to access our on-line forum for ongoing support.

This workshop runs as an Open Course and can also be provided in house.

OPTION 2: TWELVE-MONTH TAILORED MENTORING PROGRAMME

If risk management is a critical business issue for your organisation and a key part of your objectives, then our mentoring programme could be the option for you. It focuses on making good decisions around risk, protecting value in your business and making the most of opportunities, while taking others with you. This is aimed at directors, senior risk specialists and senior members of project management offices.

This programme provides just in time mentoring, focusing on your work and issues with someone who has taken time to understand your context. Over a year, you work one-to-one with Penny and Ruth. You will have support to build and sustain your risk management progress and the chance to deal with real issues as they arise. By joining this programme, you will also learn from your peers what works in other organisations.

We will invite you to join us for one-day workshops, three times a year, to build relationships with the other participants and to practise techniques for face-to-face groups. Apart from these days, your participation will not require travel. Each month, we provide a group module with a virtual seminar for all participants, as well as individual mentoring. This means that you can participate in the programme without taking out big chunks of your valuable time. Each seminar will focus on a different aspect of facilitating risk management.

You can find out more about these programmes at:

www.facilitatingrisk.com/programmes

Foreword

DAVID HILLSON

Managing risk is a challenge for many reasons. There are lots of barriers to effective risk management, including organisational, practical, procedural and personal. As a result many people don't bother with it, or if they do then they see it as a necessary chore or bureaucratic overhead. Too much so-called 'risk management' involves simply ticking boxes, going through the motions, attending risk workshops and review meetings, and getting it over with as quickly as possible so we can return to the real job. Whatever this is, it is not managing risk.

There are many ways to overcome the barriers to managing risk properly. One of the most effective is to use a skilled facilitator. As Ruth and Penny explain early in this book, the word facilitator has its roots in the Latin *facilis* meaning easy. So the facilitator's role is to make things easier for others, helping them to achieve their goals as efficiently as possible. A good facilitator understands the barriers and has proven tools and techniques for dealing with them.

Facilitation skills are helpful in a wide range of settings, but they have particular value when we are dealing with risk. If risk is defined in the way that Ruth and Penny recommend, as 'uncertainty that matters', then both the inherent uncertainty and the potential for significant consequences are likely to make people cautious in the way they approach risk. The risk workshop is not just another meeting, since we need to get it right if we are to identify the real risks that we face. Risk Registers require careful consideration as they indicate the areas requiring particular focused attention and action. Risk responses are not distractions from real work, but they define what needs to be done in order to minimise avoidable problems and maximise achievable benefits. Risk reports are important as they tell people about what is coming and what they need to do to get ready. In short, risk management matters and we need to get it right.

In this short guide, we find out how a skilled facilitator can help people who want and need to manage risk. While the focus is on the risk workshop, other aspects are covered where facilitation can provide useful direction and support. But where can we find a competent facilitator? And if I want to develop my own facilitation skills, what do I need to know? The best way to learn how to do something is to spend time with people who know how to do it. A close second is for them to tell you their secrets. That's why this short book is so valuable.

I've watched Ruth and Penny in action as they work with groups in various settings. I've been impressed at how they get alongside people, make them feel relaxed and at ease, and guide the group towards achieving their aims in a way that delivers results while still allowing them to have appropriate fun. I've found myself wishing I could do what Ruth and Penny do, and wondering how they learnt to do it so well. Now we know, as they share some of their insights in this book. These include basic facilitation skills of course, but they also show us how to apply these to the challenge of managing risk, particularly in the setting of a risk workshop.

For many years I've been telling people that risk management isn't hard, for two reasons. First, they assume that it is a 'hard discipline' because it involves statistics, analysis and a rigorous approach, when the reality is that risk is managed by people not processes or techniques. And second, people think that risk management is 'hard' because it is difficult to do, when done properly it should be an easy and intuitive process. So risk management should not be hard, because it involves soft skills and it should be easy. This book addresses both of these aspects, reminding us that the risk process is essentially people-centred and that skilled facilitation can make it easy. Anything that makes it easier for people to manage risk effectively is a good thing, and I welcome this book as a significant contribution to that end.

Dr David Hillson, The Risk Doctor
Petersfield, Hampshire, UK

Review of
A Short Guide to Facilitating Risk Management

Risk meetings don't have to be boring: *A Short Guide to Facilitating Risk Management* is the book that risk managers have been waiting for. It provides practical guidance on facilitating risk workshops, and making risk management happen outside of the workshop setting as well. Dotted throughout with cartoons, the emphasis is on practical guidance for getting things done without suffocating those poor souls who have to attend risk reviews.

The book provides a clear introduction to tackling risk (including opportunities) in a fun, professional way, with the aim of gaining consensus. It's pragmatic and practical, with real-life examples to show how risk management can become ingrained in the day-to-day management of initiatives in your organisation.

Elizabeth Harrin, author of *Project Management in the Real World* and Head of IT Programme Delivery, Spire Healthcare

Acknowledgements

We're sure that every author has many people to thank genuinely.

The list of people to thank for this book is extensive. This is because we have used the questions, stories and insights from so many practitioners working with risk management in business. They've helped us shape the structure and content of what we have written, both in this book and the accompanying website www.facilitatingrisk.com. We wanted the book to be *directly* relevant to readers, so didn't want to assume what those readers might think. So a big thank you to all those who have contributed their thoughts over the past year. We can't name everyone individually because there are too many people, but you know who you are.

We will, though, name three organisations who gave us the opportunity to meet groups of risk facilitators at special events: the Association for Project Management, the British Computer Society and the International Institute for Business Analysis UK Chapter.

We are particularly grateful to three risk facilitators who have allowed us to share their stories in detail: Vivien and Anna in Chapter 3 and Tony, along with his alien invaders, in Chapter 5.

Thank you! We know you are doing a great job and it has been good to share some of your success in this book.

Two other people have contributed a huge amount of their time to make this book so much better than we could have created on our own:

First, Vanessa Randle, whose illustrations have brought the text to life for us, and hopefully for you too. Vanessa retains copyright of all the images we have used.

Second, Malcolm Pullan who has pored over every chapter and has made the book much clearer as a result: removing jargon, rephrasing ideas and giving us a different perspective.

Then there's the team at Gower: Jonathan Norman for seeing the potential for the title as part of the Short Guide series and the whole team for their support.

Our friend and colleague David Hillson is mentioned a number of times throughout the text as his work has been such an influence on us. We are grateful that he agreed to write the Foreword and add his thoughts to ours through this section.

And finally, our families. They have encouraged us to keep going even when they'd rather have us all to themselves: through many a late night editing session (Ruth) or writing chapters on holiday when it was too rainy to venture out (Penny). So to end this long list of thanks, we dedicate this book, with our love, to Malcolm, Kathleen and Charlotte Pullan and Fred, Joshua and Helen Murray-Webster.

(1) Introduction

The success of organisations relies on making good decisions in risky and important situations. Most organisations have a defined risk management process to help them do this. Unfortunately, far too many of these processes don't deliver value. Although they are almost always logically correct, they tend not to take into account the influence of people. This book is designed to help you deliver results using risk management processes that work with and through people.

WHO IS THIS BOOK FOR?

This book is for all those who want to make sound decisions in important but risky situations: people who need to work with groups to identify, prioritise and respond to risks, and who wish to deliver value.

Does this apply to you? Maybe you have one of these job titles?

- Operations manager;

- Project or programme manager;

- Business analyst;

- Risk facilitator or manager;

- Internal or external consultant;

- Director;

- Health and safety manager; or

- HR professional.

But in truth, your job title does not matter. The only thing that matters is that you are involved with a risk management process in some way. If you are, you're likely to plan and run meetings or workshops where risks are discussed. You probably also give advice to others and coordinate people. In short, your role is to get risk management to work through other people. Throughout this book, we will use the term 'risk facilitator' to describe people who carry out such tasks.

Are meetings and workshops that focus on risk different? We believe they are, and that's why we've written this book. When groups discuss risk, they are trying to predict the future in a way that is as rational as possible, yet we know that human beings are complex and perceive risk differently. This means that what groups decide is often not rational. Some would say that when people talk about risks they are predictably irrational (Ariely, 2008). That's what makes facilitating risk management such an interesting challenge.

WHAT WILL YOU GAIN FROM READING THIS BOOK?

This book is designed to be a helpful companion to you as you manage risk. It covers five main areas:

1. AVOIDING PITFALLS

In this book, we've identified a whole host of traps for the unwary risk facilitator. These are the pitfalls that we've had to overcome ourselves and we've helped our clients with. By reading this book, especially Chapter 6, you'll know what to avoid and, more importantly, *how*. We trust that you'll be better prepared, able to use your knowledge with groups, avoiding skewed results.

2. UNDERSTANDING RISK MANAGEMENT

Groups involved in risk management need to understand what they're working on, but what level of detail do they need to go to? Chapter 2 provides a broad overview of the field of risk management, which includes the human elements. Use this to refresh your own understanding and decide what's appropriate to share with your groups.

3. UNDERSTANDING YOUR ROLE

Whether risk facilitation is just a small part of your job or takes up 100 per cent of your time, Chapter 3 will give you an overview of the skills you need. Stories from successful risk facilitators show how they've delivered results inside their organisations. You'll gain ideas on how best to develop your own skills, as well as possible development paths for your organisation.

4. TRIED AND TESTED TIPS FOR EACH STEP OF THE RISK MANAGEMENT PROCESS

Chapter 4 includes each step of the risk management process, showing how you can break it down into simple steps. We provide proven practices for each step, showing how you can use the right mix of workshops, small groups and individual work to keep people engaged and to get results from start to finish.

5. RUNNING RISK WORKSHOPS

Chapter 5 covers the whole area of making workshops work. It gives a range of practical tips to help you get the best from your groups when they're working together, both face-to-face and virtually.

Above all, this book is a practical, quick read. It's full of tips that you can put into practice straight away, confident that they are based on practical experience, as well as research. In addition to our own experience, you'll see real life stories from other risk facilitators and hear the risk management pitfalls encountered by hundreds of people.

WHY READ THIS BOOK NOW?

With the global economy recovering as we write this book, there's a focus on risk. Many feel that the credit crunch of the late 2000s was a result of poor, uncontrolled risk management and an attitude of risk seeking in banks all over the world.

Despite this, books on risk and conferences seem to focus on the risk management process – what to do when. There is a growing realisation that process alone won't make risk management work and that skilled facilitation of risk is needed as well.

Another driver is that facilitation is maturing as a discipline with much practical advice available to help risk professionals.

We met and realised that, between us, we have a rare combination of skills and experience. Ruth's books on risk attitude with David Hillson and her detailed knowledge of risk management complimented Penny's wide experience of facilitation really well, and this book was born.

OVER TO YOU

This book is designed to help you to tap into the latest understanding of risk management and apply many practical ideas and tips within your work and organisation. Please let us know how the ideas and tips work for you. We'd welcome your input and any changes you would suggest for future editions. You can contact us via the website that accompanies this book, www.facilitatingrisk.com.

REFERENCES

Ariely, D. (2008) *Predictably Irrational: The Hidden Forces that Shape our Decisions*, New York: HarperCollins.

② What is Risk Management?

In this chapter we want to explore what risk management means for practitioners. If risk management is to work, then there are some things that must be in place – we'll point out what they are.

People and their organisations can often become fixated on formal risk management methods, process and tools. This is clear from looking at the topics covered in conferences or by reading magazines and books on the subject.

Organisations have spent a small fortune setting up methods, processes, tools and training; but these things alone do not enable great risk management practice. Risk management is difficult in practice because it relies on getting groups of people to agree on how to manage things in the future, things that only *may* happen. It is often counter-intuitive for people to spend their valuable time *now* considering things that only *might* happen in the future. Getting groups of people to agree how to do this is even more challenging. Different people have different perceptions, pre-conceptions and hang-ups about what might happen and what matters most. Facilitation is really important here in order to engage and encourage people with different viewpoints to work together effectively.

The chapter is split it into five sections. We will:

1. Give you an overview of the words people use in *describing risk management*, both informally and formally.

2. Outline for you the *fundamentals of risk assessment*.

3. Show why *human beings and their opinions matter*.

4. Help you to understand the essential steps in *responding to risks wisely*.

5. Provide some tips on *keeping risk management alive*.

DESCRIBING RISK MANAGEMENT

Although humans have been managing risk forever, there are still good reasons why some sort of process is needed in organisations. First and foremost, though, think about risk management as a natural human process. If you reflect on what you and others do naturally, it can help to find ways of making risk management successful in work and group situations.

People are all great risk managers, or we wouldn't have come so far along life's pathway, largely intact and unscathed.

So why do organisations need to develop a systematic, formal process for risk management? There are two primary reasons:

1. To help to make plans and forecasts about the future as robust as possible. Plans include bids for external work, bids for internal funding and setting expectations about results. Plans outline what will be done, to what standards, when and for how much.

2. To make a connection between all the personal intuitive assessments of risk that exist to try to establish a common understanding of how to proceed across the organisation.

The need for a consistent, shared and organised approach in organisations has brought a degree of formality to a natural process. As members of organisations we have little option but to go with this, but it's good to hold on to the knowledge that each one of us is a naturally capable risk manager.

We can't talk about risk without using words like chance and consequence:

- What's the chance that *x* will happen?

- If I take the chance, what might the consequence be?

This simple concept can seem more complicated when words such as probability or likelihood are used instead of chance; or when impact or effect are used to mean the same as consequence.

People also talk about *risk, a risk, the risk*, what is *at risk*, that's *risky*. There are many parts of speech all referring to things that might happen that would matter to us if they did.

Processes developed by professional bodies, regulators and standards organisations have tried to define terms using a common language. You can judge from reviewing Table 2.1 whether this has been successful. The table lists many of the current standards and guides relating to risk management, along with the words they use to describe risk, and the risk management process.

In addition to those risk management standards referenced in the table, yet more exist. These include documents that describe the language used for example in financial services; or subject specialisms such as health and safety, business continuity or insurance. There is also national and international guidance and legislation that requires companies to manage risk at a corporate level such as the UK Corporate Governance Code, the US legislation known as Sarbanes Oxley or SOx, or the European Basel Accord (currently Basel III). If you want to know more about these then a Google™ search will help you out.

So given the natural, yet organised approach to the management of risk at work, what are the fundamentals of a risk assessment?

Table 2.1   Comparison of risk management standards

	Definition of risk	Risk management process	Unique aspects and emphasis
ISO31000: 2009 Risk Management Principles and Guidelines	The effect of uncertainty on objectives.	• Communicate and consult • Establish context • Risk identification • Risk assessment • Risk evaluation • Risk treatment • Monitor and review	• Principles led • Focus on the whole enterprise • Clearly links risk management with decision-making
Guide to the Project Management Body of Knowledge [PMBoK®] – Fourth edition (2008)	An uncertain event or condition that, if it occurs, has a positive or negative effect on a project's objectives.	• Risk management planning • Risk identification • Qualitative risk analysis • Quantitative risk analysis • Risk response planning • Risk monitoring and control	• Strong process orientation (inputs/tools and techniques/outputs) • Addresses opportunities as well as threats
Project Risk Analysis and Management [PRAM] Guide – Second edition (2004)	**Risk event** An uncertain event or set of circumstances that, should it or they occur, would have an effect on the achievement of one or more of the project's objectives. **Project risk** The exposure of stakeholders to the consequences of variations in outcome.	• Initiate • Identify • Assess • Plan responses • Implement responses • Manage process	• Includes chapters on benefits of managing risks (2), establishing a risk management organisation (5), behavioural aspects (6), and implementation/application issues (7) • Addresses threats and opportunities • Defines risk at two levels; risk event and project risk

	Definition of risk	Risk management process	Unique aspects and emphasis
Management of Risk – Guidance for Practitioners (M_o_R) (2010)	Uncertainty of outcome (whether positive opportunity or negative threat). It is the combination of the chance of an event and its consequences.	• Identify context • Identify the risks • Identify probable risk owners • Evaluate the risks • Plan suitable responses to risks • Implement responses • Gain assurance about effectiveness • Embed into culture and review	• Applicable to strategic, programme, project and operational risk • Part of a larger suite of methods
IRM/ALARM/ AIRMIC Risk Management Standard (2002)	The combination of the probability of an event and its consequences.	• The organisation's strategic objectives • Risk identification • Risk description • Risk estimation • Risk evaluation • Risk reporting • Risk treatment • Monitoring and review	• Applicable to business and projects • Link to organisation strategic management • Chapter (9) devoted to roles of various functions in the organisation
Risk Analysis and Management for Projects [RAMP] – Second edition (2005)	A threat (or opportunity) which could affect adversely (or favourably) achievement of the objective's of an investment.	• Process launch • Plan and initiate risk review • Identify risks • Evaluate risks • Devise measures for responding to risks	• Considers opportunities as well as threats • Focus is on whole life assets, with emphasis on capital projects

	Definition of risk	Risk management process	Unique aspects and emphasis
		• Assess residual risks and decide whether to continue • Plan responses to residual risks • Communicate risk response strategy and response plan • Implement strategy and plans • Control risks • Process close-down	
BS IEC 62198:2001 – Project risk management – Application guidelines (2002)	Combination of the probability of an event occurring and its consequences on project objectives.	• Establishing the context • Risk identifications • Risk assessment • Risk treatment • Risk review and monitoring • Post-project	• Originated as part of dependability standard • Focus on projects with technological content
BS6079-3:2000 – Project management – Part 3: Guide to the risk management of business related project risk (2000)	Uncertainty inherent in plans and the possibility of something happening (i.e. a contingency) that can affect the possibility of achieving business or project goals.	• Context • Risk identification • Risk analysis • Risk evaluation • Risk treatment • Communicate/monitor and review/update plans	• Focus on link to business objectives and strategy • Roles of perception and stakeholder analysis

Source: Updated by Murray-Webster from an original in Hillson and Simon, 2007.

FUNDAMENTALS OF RISK ASSESSMENT

WHAT IS RISK?

One of the first things to think about is the difference between uncertainty and risk. Uncertainty and risk are different. Many things are uncertain, not all of them are risks. Uncertainties only become risks when they could affect our objectives. 'Risks are uncertainties that matter' (Hillson and Murray-Webster, 2007).

It is also really important not to become confused between risks and issues. Issues are problems that are happening now. There is nothing uncertain about them at all. Issues may be causes of risks, so there is a link between them – but it's critical that they're not managed in the same way.

RISK – GOOD, BAD OR BOTH?

Contrary to English dictionary definitions, risks are not necessarily negative – threats to our objectives. Some of the situations that are uncertain would result in a beneficial outcome should they occur.

For example, the currency exchange rate when I go on holiday may be more favourable to me than the rate I used when budgeting. To get the best out of risk management it's important to focus not just on potential *problems, but also potential opportunities* – downsides and upsides.

HOW MUCH RISK CAN YOU TOLERATE?

It's also really important to know how much risk you are comfortable with. This applies to you as an individual as well as to your project, or department. Practitioners who talk about this concept use three slightly different, but linked terms – risk capacity, risk appetite and risk tolerance.

So you'll need to answer questions such as: 'How much risk do we have the capacity and resources to bear? And 'How "hungry" are we for risk within that capacity?' 'Are we able to make some risky choices because the potential prize is greater than the potential loss?' Or 'Have we taken on enough risk already and don't have an appetite, or a capacity for more?' Answering these questions will allow you to define the tolerances that we are prepared to accept for a particular activity.

*A simple home example might be related to a family holiday in the sun. Most of us are not likely to have the **capacity** and resources to book alternative flights if we miss the one we are booked on. On that*

understanding, we are not likely to have much of an **appetite** *for taking risks that would cause us to miss our flight, so we set* **tolerances** *around the time we leave for the airport that provide us some contingency. We may spend too long in airports (and my children would say that provides the opportunity for shopping), but we don't take too many chances related to the primary objective.*

A critical first step in risk management is to define the organisation's risk capacity, risk appetite, and therefore the risk tolerances for the work they're doing. This is an activity that must be done by the senior management of the organisational unit in question. That could be the Executive Management Team for a whole organisation, or it might be a Departmental Team, Programme Sponsoring Group, or similar. Helping senior teams through this first decision-making process is a task where experienced risk facilitators can help enormously.

WHAT'S RISKY AND WHY?

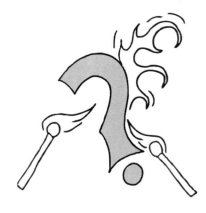

Too often organisations have lists of risks where the associated descriptions tell us very little about the situation. If you can understand the cause of a risk, you may be able to avoid it entirely (for a threat) or exploit it (for an opportunity).

It is vitally important to describe risks well if we are to make good assessments of their relative priority. Think about describing risks in a way that distinguishes between the cause (a fact), the risk event (which isn't a fact)and the impact on objectives (why it matters).

An example of a positive risk (potential opportunity) might be:

- because business is slower this year than last year and staff have more time,

- the company may be able to generate greater brand awareness by exploiting new e-marketing skills,

- resulting in increased sales.

An example of a negative risk (threat) might be:

- because business is slower this year than last year and staff have more time,

- staff may become de-motivated and less effective,

- resulting in an accelerated decline in sales.

Can you see the cause, the risk event and the effect in each of these? Being able to turn vague expressions of risk into specific risk descriptions, as shown in the examples, is a fundamental step towards effective risk assessment.

Another good reason for describing risks well is to encourage people to think about *why* their situation is risky in the first place.

With some risks we can calculate the odds with certainty – situations like playing the lottery and other games of pure chance. Risks in business are fundamentally different. When playing the lottery, it's possible to calculate the exact chance of winning. In business, there is no situation that is a game of pure chance because there are always other factors that we don't know enough about, yet are influential. When situations are ambiguous it is impossible to calculate probabilities with precision – we can only make our most educated guess. This means that judgements about risk are highly subjective.

HOW MUCH DOES EACH RISK MATTER?

Even though judgements about the chance of a particular risk occurring are subjective, we still need to make these judgements so we can prioritise risks and decide which ones warrant management rather than leaving the situation to chance. Prioritisation is typically done by combining the assessment of probability (the chance that the uncertainty will become fact) with a judgement of how much the risk would impact on our objectives. Here we are guessing too. However, we can make these guesses more 'educated' by defining specific criteria for what makes a risk on a particular objective high, medium or low.

Because human assessments of probability and impact are educated guesses, it's important to avoid relying on any one individual's opinion. Where there's relevant data that can be used it should be – but often data about the past isn't that relevant in predicting the future. For example, just because the last three summers have been wet it doesn't help us predict the weather this summer. We need to prioritise risks as objectively as possible – on the basis of their likelihood and the scale of their impact. Some organisations present the prioritisation of individual risks visually on a grid – often called a probability/impact grid, a risk assessment matrix, a heat map, or other similar title. Other organisations use a simple calculation of expected monetary value (EMV) to cost each risk, allowing a financial prioritisation. This is done by estimating the most likely cost of the impact should the risk event occur, then calculating a percentage of this impact cost based on the estimated probability. This is not a precise science, but allows risks to be compared using a monetary value.

HOW RISKY IS THIS SITUATION?

When each of the identified risks has been assessed for probability and impact, you have a prioritisation based on the chance of each risk event happening and the consequences if it did. This list is usually structured as a risk log or risk register.

Such a list is useful of course, but you can't judge the overall riskiness of the situation from a simple list of discrete risks. To assess total risk relies on using techniques that allow you to look at the combined effect of discrete risks on the overall objectives. The outputs from this analysis show how much the objectives are exposed to risk, and are useful for a number of purposes. These include:

- making provision for a contingency budget (risk reserve);

- shaping bids – either for internal funding or to win client work; and

- discussing confidence levels in estimates with stakeholders.

Some organisations use sophisticated modelling and simulation techniques to support their risk-based decision-making. Describing the mathematics underpinning such techniques is out of scope of this book on facilitation, however the techniques rely on the availability of good input data to help people make appropriate decisions. Unfortunately, Penny and Ruth see far too many situations where 'garbage in' gives 'garbage out' no matter how sophisticated the process in-between. What's even more dangerous is where people believe that the 'garbage out' is good information! The risk facilitator can play a vital role in organisations that use risk-modelling techniques. They can help the decision-making team to challenge the assumptions underpinning the data and to carry out analyses that provide good information on which to base risky and important business decisions.

HUMAN BEINGS AND THEIR OPINIONS MATTER

Although risk management is a natural skill for most human beings – there is a complicating factor. Risk is about perception. Ruth's perception of what is risky is different from Penny's. Put ten people in a room and present them with the same information and you will get ten different views of what the risks are, how likely they are to occur and how much they'd matter if they did. So although the risk management process is largely common sense, it is not easy to get shared views. Adding more people increases the range of views!

Ruth's work with David Hillson on understanding and managing risk attitude (Hillson and Murray-Webster, 2007, Murray-Webster and Hillson, 2008) explains the large number of factors that have the power to influence perceptions. A summary table is included in Appendix A of this chapter. These perceptions affect assessments of risk because they determine the choices that different people adopt in risky situations. One example is the impact of positive experience on the perception of risks. If I've enjoyed doing something risky in the past, I'm likely to downplay the risks in a future, similar situation and believe that I can manage anything adverse that may occur. The reverse also applies. If we have no experience, or have had a bad experience in the past, most people are likely to be more cautious in future. This is one of a huge number of influences on human perception of risk and riskiness. More will be explored later in the book when we look at pitfalls, and how facilitation helps, but it can be useful to think about the influences on perception of risk as falling into three groups as shown below.

The three groups of influences (called the 'triple strand' in Murray-Webster and Hillson's work) combine so that at the point where each of us makes a judgement about a risk, the strands are tightly intertwined, making it quite difficult to distinguish the particular influences that have led to our opinion. In situations that are particularly risky and important, people, or teams of people, need to have the skills to unpick the triple strand and check that the chosen response to the risk is appropriate in the situation. Some people have the personal skills to test their assumptions in this way, or to help their team do this. Many don't and benefit greatly from support from a skilled facilitator who demonstrates the qualities shown below. We have found that great facilitators can 'read' a situation well and through a combination of seeing, hearing and feeling can work out how to balance the needs of the situation.

RISK ATTITUDE LABELS

It is common for people to use labels such as risk averse, risk tolerant or risk seeking to describe the risk attitude of people, groups, organisations and even nations. What do these labels mean in practice?

We adopt the definition of risk attitude from Ruth's

books with David Hillson, that is, chosen response to a risk, driven by perception. Risk attitudes, held by individuals or groups, are situational. We each have different chosen responses to different risks at different times. Penny and Ruth can both agree that they are much more risk averse when it comes to taking risks with their children's safety than they are when making business choices. But what does risk averse mean? Simply it is the degree of the comfort with the perceived level of risk. A risk-averse attitude is relatively uncomfortable with the perceived level of risk so there is motivation to try to make the situation more certain. A risk-seeking attitude is relatively comfortable with the perceived level of risk so there is no motivation to create more certainty. Risk tolerant and risk neutral attitudes are also described below in Table 2.2.

Table 2.2   Risk attitude labels

Term	Definition
Risk Averse	Uncomfortable with uncertainty, desire to avoid or reduce threats and exploit opportunities to remove uncertainty. Would be unhappy with an uncertain outcome.
Risk Seeking	Comfortable with uncertainty, no desire to avoid or reduce threats or to exploit opportunities to remove uncertainty. Would be happy with an uncertain outcome.
Risk Tolerant	Tolerant of uncertainty, no strong desire to respond to threats or opportunities in any way. Could tolerate an uncertain outcome if necessary.
Risk Neutral	Uncomfortable with uncertainty in the long term so prepared to take whatever short-term actions are necessary to deliver a certain long-term outcome.

Source: Murray-Webster and Hillson, 2008.

RESPONDING TO RISKS WISELY

Identifying risks associated with those objectives that matter most to us, describing them well and prioritising them are all important parts of the process. When you've done this you can put together plans and bids for work or funding that address risk explicitly. Some organisations stop here and leave the risks to chance, knowing what they are but not doing anything to try to manage them, or increase their beneficial impact on objectives. That's risk assessment, with no risk management.

There are other options, typically described as risk response strategies in the books and guides, but colloquially often called 'risk mitigation' by practitioners.

NOT JUST ABOUT MITIGATION!

At this point it's worth stating that, in Ruth and Penny's opinion, using the term mitigation in all cases is not that helpful. Mitigation, derived from the old English verb to 'soften' and defined in dictionaries as 'to reduce, makes less severe or render less harsh or hostile' is *one* approach to dealing with a downside risk or threat. But there are others as described below – and of course lots of things you can do to make positive risks *more* likely and *more* beneficial should they occur.

So what are the essential steps when deciding whether or not to act to respond to a particular risk?

OWNERSHIP

The first thing that must be done is to make sure that the risk has an owner – a named person who is best placed to make decisions about how to manage the risk. When talking to practitioners during the writing of this book, Ruth and Penny have heard many concerns about the lack of clear ownership for specific risks. This is of concern. If a risk is real and worthy of assessment and management then a person who cares (or is paid to care!) about the impact the risk could have on objectives must take ownership of that risk. The risk owner is then the person who takes the decisions about *if and how* to respond to the risk.

These are the options open to you as a risk owner:

- Take the risk.

- Prepare a plan B.

- Treat the risk.

- Share (not transfer).

- Make it certain.

Each option is described here.

Take the risk

You could accept the risk. Accepting a risk doesn't mean doing nothing, as every risk needs to be monitored to make sure it doesn't creep up and surprise you, but it does mean not spending any time and money now to try to make the situation more certain. Often called the '*accept*' strategy – it's all about being willing to let the uncertainty play out.

Prepare a plan B

Accepting the risk without any preparation for what you'd do if the risk did occur can be simply irresponsible, especially if the risk will have a highly positive or highly negative impact on your objectives. One response strategy that is not often described, but we believe is a very natural approach, is to *accept the risk – for now* – but spend a little time and effort putting in place a 'plan B'. A 'plan B' is a simple way of referring to what you will do *if* the risk materialises, for example, having spare clothes in your hand-luggage in case your checked luggage doesn't arrive with you in time for an important meeting. Some of the standards and guides talk about plan Bs as contingent plans, fall-back plans or real-options. Real-options are interesting since they buy you flexibility to decide whether to spend money now or at a later date – but with the knowledge that the plan B is in place. We think this response option is an instinctive one used often in our lives, but is not considered enough in work situations.

Both the 'take' or 'accept' strategy, and the 'prepare' strategy as described above don't tend to require large investments of time and money now. Other strategies are likely to require bigger immediate investments and so they need to be thought through carefully, and costed so that the organisation knows that the response delivers value for money. Some people find it very counter-intuitive to spend time and money now on a situation that may not happen anyway, however the whole business case for risk management is that overall it's cheaper to prevent than cure.

Treat the risk

For some significant risks, the best option may be to try to reduce the uncertainty in some way. Treating a negative threat is where the word mitigate applies! You are trying to *reduce* probability, reduce impact or both. Treating a positive, potential opportunity is usually referred to as the *enhance* strategy and involves trying to increase probability, impact or both.

Share (not transfer)

One way of treating a risk is to share the risk with others. This can be done in the supply chain, sharing a risk with a customer or supplier, so the impact of any loss/pain or gain is not with one party. For example, if bad weather prevents progress on the building of a new extension at home, the costs of paying the staff could be shared between you and your builder. We like the word *share* as an alternative to the word transfer that is often used. Although insurance can be seen as a form of risk transfer, we argue you can never transfer all the risk to another party. Someone else might pay the costs if the risk occurs, but inevitably there'll be some impact on your objectives too, for example extra time. This point is all too clear in Ruth's mind having spent a whole weekend sorting out her cellar following a flood. The insurance paid for damage, but not Ruth's time in sorting out all the messy bits!

Sharing risk is a good thing to do and lots of contracts are now set up on a pain share/gain share basis to do just that. *It is important to beware of the 'transfer' word* – particularly when working with suppliers and customers in the supply chain. As noted by official bodies such as the UK National Audit Office (2010), attempting to transfer risk in the supply chain tends to destroy trust and can result in people padding their estimates more and more. Smart organisations are starting to realise that. Although risk transfer is a potential option in some situations, it should only be done with eyes open to the potential consequences of doing so.

As highlighted in all of response strategies mentioned so far, a *residual risk* remains if the response strategy has been to take the risk, prepare a plan B, treat the risk, share the risk or transfer the risk. Most of these generic responses will have changed either the assessment of probability, the assessment of impact, or both. There will still be a residual risk that means that there is still some probability of the threat or opportunity having an impact on objectives.

Make it certain

You could argue the first thing to consider is whether or not you can do something to eliminate the risk altogether – so there is no residual risk. This is one of the reasons why describing risks in a three-part way – the cause, the risk event and the effect – is so powerful. If you can get rid of the cause of a threat, the risk has gone. If you can make the cause of an opportunity completely certain, you've got it. Making a potential problem or a potential opportunity certain is often called the terminate option. You may find it more helpful to talk about *avoiding* threats and *exploiting* opportunities. Sometimes it might cost lots of time and money to do this, yet it's still worth it.

Sometimes just thinking about the situation in a different way can have the same result for no additional cost.

And be careful!

The trick with all these response strategies is to avoid planning actions that would make the situation even more risky. The technical term for this is secondary risk. In common parlance we'd talk about not 'jumping from the frying pan into the fire' or 'throwing the baby out with the bath-water'. An example might be reducing the risk of your children becoming injured in the park by not letting them play outside with their friends at all. In avoiding one risk (your children being injured, or worse), you introduce bigger risks associated with health, socialisation and general 'street-wise' skills. (Waiton and Baird, 2007). So when you've planned risk responses, make sure you add any secondary threats or opportunities to the risk register and assess the chance and impact of them occurring in the usual way. This way you can make sure that risk responses don't have unintended consequences.

KEEPING RISK MANAGEMENT ALIVE

Any risk assessment and management plan is only a snapshot in time. As the work progresses, new information might come to light, situations change or new people join the team. The situation is dynamic not static, so risk management needs to keep pace.

The best type of risk management is where the whole team, top to bottom, lives the process. Where this happens, discussions about potential opportunities and potential problems are part

of day-to-day conversations as well as being embedded in the formal governance and decision-making processes. The risk register is 'alive' and the team embrace the process because they know it adds considerable value.

The worst type of risk management is the 'tick-box' compliance type, where risk registers are only completed or updated just before an audit, or when the customer asks to see it. This sort of behaviour devalues what can be a massively useful process. We've observed that when 'lip-service' is paid to the risk management process the result is a sapping of energy and a creation of a cynicism that is difficult for organisations to break.

One point of view is that a compliance mentality to risk management is of no value – possibly worse than doing nothing at all and leaving the risk to chance. Why? Because leaving it all to chance does not incur the costs of 'pretending' to do risk management. For the costs of applying risk management to deliver a return on investment, a supportive culture is required.

In the final analysis, many individuals manage risk intuitively – they always have and will. However, in situations where there is a 'tick-box' approach, the organisation is unlikely to get any of the formal benefits, and so may as well spend its time doing something else.

For organisations that can overcome a compliance mentality and do risk management well, the benefits from risk management are three-fold:

1. *Less waste* (problems that could have been foreseen, missed opportunities, re-work and hassle).

2. *More confidence* (in plans, forecasts and relationships because there are fewer surprises).

3. *Better decisions* (because decision-making is based on the best possible information – not just about what is, but about what might be).

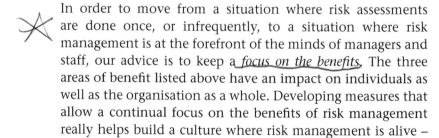

In order to move from a situation where risk assessments are done once, or infrequently, to a situation where risk management is at the forefront of the minds of managers and staff, our advice is to keep a *focus on the benefits*. The three areas of benefit listed above have an impact on individuals as well as the organisation as a whole. Developing measures that allow a continual focus on the benefits of risk management really helps build a culture where risk management is alive – with 'evergreen' risk registers and proactive behaviours.

Developing suitable performance-based measures that show how risk management helps is sometimes a challenge for organisations. One of the challenges to overcome is the fact that a problem avoided isn't very visible. There's nothing tangible to measure when something doesn't happen. However trends can be measured, for example, waste can be *tracked over time*. With improved risk management there should be a downward trend in the cost of waste. Remember the simple calculation of expected monetary value (EMV) for each risk, explained earlier in this chapter. Many organisations use this to track how well the overall riskiness of the work is reduced over time. Another way is to track time spent on re-work, or other wasteful actions that could have been foreseen and prevented by proactive risk management.

Confidence and the strength of relationships can also be tracked through customer and staff surveys, or 'voice of the client' focus groups. Clients who lack confidence will tend to micro-manage, or be overly contractual about issues. The same is true for internal managers. I'm sure we can all think of how our behaviour is affected when there is confidence in a relationship, as opposed to no confidence. It is to be expected that behaviour will be influenced by surprises, irrespective of whether they are nasty ones that hurt (actually or metaphorically), or the knowledge of a missed opportunity. What effective risk management can enable is confidence that surprises will be minimised and therefore relationships flourish and grow within teams across businesses and supply chains. This is because people will be working well together to anticipate potential problems and opportunities. Their confidence and success will grow as the number of issues and problems diminishes.

Whatever indicators or measures you use to keep the focus on the benefits of risk management; the key from our point of view is that at least some of these are measuring trends. Trends give you information on the degree to which risk management is dynamic, alive, well and adding tangible value over time. Taking the time to gather this data really helps to move risk management away from the 'tick-box' compliance arena that so many practitioners complain about.

SUMMARY

In this chapter, we've explained how risk management comes naturally to human beings and is a key part of general life as well as business. We've also outlined the steps in the risk process and the key things to be aware of. Although, at one level, good risk management seems to be common sense, experience says that it isn't common practice. We've covered a whole range of complicating factors that explain why this is so. You'll need to be aware of these to be a great risk facilitator and get the best out of groups.

So what does it take to be a great risk facilitator? Chapter 3 describes the role of the facilitator in general then Chapter 4 will show the many ways in which facilitators can support the risk process described in this chapter, in different organisational settings and contexts. Many people associate risk facilitation with risk workshops. We argue that the risk workshop is only one part of risk facilitation, albeit an important one. Workshops are the subject of Chapter 5. Chapter 6 then lists the challenges that practitioners have told us they experience. We respond to each of these pitfalls before closing this book with our ten golden guidelines for risk facilitators in Chapter 7.

REFERENCES

Hillson, D.A. and Murray-Webster, R. (2007) *Understanding and Managing Risk Attitude,* (2nd edition), Aldershot: Gower.

Hillson, D.A. and Simon, P.W. (2007) *Practical Project Risk Management: The ATOM Methodology,* Vienna, VA: Management Concepts.

Murray-Webster, R. and Hillson, D.A. (2008) *Managing Group Risk Attitude,* Aldershot: Gower.

Waiton, S. and Baird, S. (eds) (2007) *Cotton Wool Kids? Making Sense of 'Child Safety',* Glasgow: Generation Youth Issues. Available at: www.futurecities.org.uk/articles/CottonWoolKids.pdf [accessed 3 September 2010].

National Audit Office (2010) *Delivering Multi-role Tanker Aircraft Capability* (Report HC443). Available at: http://www.nao.org.uk/publications/0910/tanker_aircraft.aspx [accessed 16 February 2011].

Appendix A Factors with the power to influence perception and risk attitude

Situational Factors	Subconscious Factors		Affective Factors
Rational Considerations	Heuristics	Cognitive Bias	Emotions and Feelings
Familiarity	**Intuition**	**Repetition Bias**	**Fear (dread, worry, concern...)**
'I've/we've done something like this before' (or)	'Feels right, I won't look for any more data'	'Undue importance given to repeated data – must be true!'	'Of consequences of something happening'
'I've/we've never done something like this before'	**Representativeness**	**Illusion of Control**	**Desire(excitement, wonder...)**
Manageability	'This must be like this other one I've seen before'	'Exaggerate personal influence, discount luck'	'Of consequences of something happening'
'I/we know what to do to manage this' (or)	**Availability**	**Illusion of Knowledge**	**Love (lust, adoration, attraction...)**
'I/we don't know what to do to manage this'	'Most recent data is most memorable' Closely linked to **reality traps** where 'too much value is attributed to existing situations, blinded by what is, cannot see what might be if could disengage from reality'	'Some knowledge or relevant experience masks what isn't known, particularly if the person feels they *should* know'	'I want it/more of it'
Proximity		**Intelligence Trap**	**Hate (dislike, disgust...)**
'If it happens it will happen soon so need to sort it now' (or)		'Ability to mentally construct and verbally reason (IQ) means that the conclusions must be correct'	'I don't want it/less of it'
'It wouldn't happen for ages, we've got time'	**Confirmation Trap**	**Optimism Bias**	**Joy (happy, carefree...)**
Personal Propinquity	'Undue confidence – selective perception, trust me, I'm a...? Can become a **self-fulfilling prophecy**'	'Delusional optimism driven by cognitive biases and/or perceived organisational pressures and norms'	'Life is good, more good things are possible'
'If it happens it would really matter to me/us personally' (or)	**Lure of Choice**		**Sadness (depressed, morbid...)**
'If it happens it would affect objectives, but it wouldn't really matter to me/us personally'	'Biased by options that include future alternative		'Life is bad, more bad things are probable'

Situational Factors	Subconscious Factors		Affective Factors
Rational Considerations	Heuristics	Cognitive Bias	Emotions and Feelings
Severity of impact 'If it happens the effect would be huge (or insignificant)' **Group Dynamics and Organisational Culture** 'The norms of how this particular group behaves'	judgements – keeping options open' **Affect Heuristic** 'Seeking pleasure, avoiding pain' **Anchoring** 'Attach illogical significance to available data, first impressions last' **Group effects, e.g. groupthink** 'We all think this way'	**Fatalism Bias** 'Ignore probabilities, focus on impact of outcomes – always optimistically, i.e. best case will happen' **Precautionary Principle** 'Ignore probabilities, focus on impact of outcomes – always pessimistically, i.e. worst case will happen' **Hindsight Bias** 'Fail to learn – I knew it all along'	

Source: Murray-Webster and Hillson, 2008.

3 The Risk Facilitator

What is a risk facilitator? It certainly isn't a common job title. However, if you aim to get the best from risk processes, work with groups to manage risk within an organisation and run risk workshops, then you are acting as one.

Making it easy

What *exactly* does the term risk facilitator mean? The root of the word 'facile' comes from the Latin 'to make easy.' So a facilitator is someone who makes something easy. A risk facilitator is someone who makes risk management work as easily as possible. They bring energy and life to what can be a dull and pedantic process.

Unfortunately, energy and life are frequently absent in risk management. Too often, we've found that risk registers are completed and then ignored. We've even found quotes such as 'Risk Identification meetings are tedious and detailed' in reference books! While this may be a very common experience, we disagree that this has to be so. Bringing risk management to life by engaging people is possible. We'll explain how you can do it and the difference it makes. We'll share stories from people who have brought risk alive inside their organisation later in this chapter.

WHAT IS FACILITATION?

Facilitation is growing as a profession in its own right and as a key skill for organisations. Why is this so? We're moving from an era of command and control into one where we need to get things done through other people, often without any line management authority. This is a challenge faced by risk facilitators. They need to get people right across their organisation to take risks seriously and to take action as a result.

Facilitation is not just a set of skills. It's also an attitude of mind, whereby we choose to do what we can to make it as easy as possible for people to achieve their outcomes. There is quite a body of information about facilitation. You can find some references at the end of this book. For an overview of facilitation of risk workshops, see Chapter 5.

Facilitators need a whole set of skills. These include being able to:

1. *Work with large, and increasingly diverse groups:* New facilitators might just work within their own teams. As they develop their skills, they will work with larger groups of people from

a wider range of areas of their organisation. Those who work with global teams, or across organisations, need to be able to handle big cultural differences across group members.

2. *Manage their own state and that of the groups they work with:* This will encourage people to tackle risks and take action. If the facilitator is tired and not interested, the group will be affected. If the group is tired and bored, the facilitator has little chance of stimulating ideas or gaining commitment to action from them. So facilitators need to have a range of tools and techniques up their sleeve to make sure that they are as effective as possible, both for themselves and for their groups. They need to be able to shift the group to a state appropriate for each task. For example, a state of positive and creative anticipation is useful when searching for opportunities. If a group is flagging, they probably won't come up with many!

3. *Work face-to-face or virtually:* Depending on whether their groups are together in one place or spread apart geographically. There are particular skills in getting the best out of a group that is working virtually. Facilitators need skills both in dealing with and using technology and also knowing how to work without the visual clues of body language and the deep relationships that people can develop when face-to-face. Virtual groups are often mixed culturally and across time zones, adding even more complexity to the facilitator's job.

4. *Deal with conflict:* People will have different viewpoints, particularly about the importance and impact of risks. This leads to disagreements. Conflict of this sort should be welcomed, rather than frowned upon. With such 'task conflict', it's good to listen to all the different viewpoints

of individuals in a group in order to build up a complete picture. Relationship conflict is a different matter. This destructive form of conflict needs to be sorted out quickly, before it destroys the trust and commitment of each person to the group. For more practical ideas on how to do this, see Chapter 5.

5. *Be familiar with a wide range of facilitation tools and techniques:* Facilitators need to have a range of tools and techniques at their fingertips and to be able to adapt these to meet the needs of the group they're working with. For example, a facilitator might start to gather information from a group by asking each person to give their input out loud. If someone starts to criticise ideas, the facilitator should change the way they gather information to something more anonymous, in order to encourage people to contribute. Some ideas for this might include writing ideas on Post-it™ notes (face-to-face) or using an anonymous survey tool (virtual). There is a wide range of media options for those using technology to support virtual teams. Virtual risk facilitators need to know which options work well and in what circumstances.

6. *Sustain participation:* The best risk facilitators keep risk alive, bringing people with them throughout the whole risk management process. With many, less experienced facilitators, this does not happen. Any initial enthusiasm fizzles out, making people much less likely to bother identifying and dealing with new risks that arise.

7. *Guide groups to outcomes:* Facilitators need to be focused on the outcome for their group. They need to guide the group using a variety of approaches to ensure that the outcome is met, tasks are completed and actions are agreed.

Facilitators need to be skilled in managing group dynamics and process as well as the skills listed above. While neutral facilitators lead groups to outcomes, this doesn't mean they deal with the actual content of discussions. A useful way to think of this uses a hamburger analogy for facilitation:

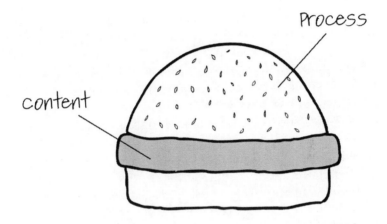

The burger represents the content of the facilitated session, the 'meat'. The bread bun around the burger represents how and when things happen to the content, that is, the process. When acting as a facilitator, you need to stay neutral and vegetarian by staying out of other people's content and concentrating on the process that brings the best result for the group. However, it's not quite this straightforward for a risk facilitator. First, you require a thorough understanding of risk management as laid out in Chapter 2. Second, you need to understand each step of the risk process and how to facilitate it from Chapter 4. Third, you have to be able to challenge the risks that people come up with. Here are some reasons why risk facilitators need to challenge their groups:

- to separate out issues (where there is no uncertainly) from real risks (which are uncertain);

- to make sure that causes of risk are separated from risk events and from the effects of those risks; and

- to challenge group dynamics that may be leading to skewed perspectives.

Unless you facilitate risk for your own team or project, you are unlikely to own the risks. You need to make sure that ownership of risk stays with the people responsible for their areas. That's one of the ways of keeping risk alive.

So, we propose a slight addition to the hamburger model for risk facilitators, adding some lettuce and slices of tomato to represent your knowledge of risk management and your ability to challenge risks. Risk facilitators are not just interested in the facilitation process as a neutral facilitator would be. They're also interested in making sure that people understand risk and that they have formulated their risks in a way that is helpful.

Facilitation process

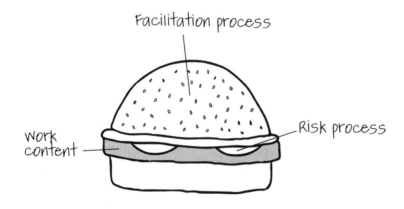

work
content

Risk process

Penny interviewed John for this book. Here's his take on the role of risk facilitator:

> *John's been facilitating risk management for years. Why? 'I suppose I have a masochistic streak,' he laughs. 'Risk is often an area no one else is interested in doing as they don't want to be labelled as negative.' John's record of delivery shows he's quite the opposite. What are his top tips for making risk management work? 'Do what it takes to get people enthused. Get momentum and keep it real. Add in structure and clear thinking, while keeping it fun. Be careful with tools. They can get in the way if they get too complex. I like yellow stickies!' Why does John think that a risk facilitator is so valuable? 'Risk management works best when you have someone who is detached from the risks and who has an absolute handle on the process.'*

WHERE IN THE ORGANISATION MIGHT YOU FIND A RISK FACILITATOR?

'Risk facilitator' is a role unlikely to be listed on an organisation chart. But those who make risk work as easily as possible within an organisation *are* risk facilitators. Where in the organisation might we find such people? Well, there are many areas. These include business continuity, financial, health and safety, environmental, security or organisational change to name just a few.

One common area to find risk facilitators is in project management. Project managers can be interested in risks to their own project, as well as helping other people with risks on their project. Business analysts are particularly interested in risks to requirements. Sometimes people inside project support offices look after the facilitation of risk across their organisation.

Other risk facilitators can be found in governance roles. Increasingly, facilitators are found within specialist risk departments at corporate level.

How much time do risk facilitators spend actually facilitating risk? Well, this can vary enormously from almost nothing, perhaps just a few hours a year, through to almost all of their time.

Risk facilitators may operate as internal consultants inside organisations. This is a role that Penny played for many years inside Mars Inc. as an internal consultant in the Effective Business Change team. One aspect of her role was to facilitate risk workshops. Another was to develop the facilitation capabilities of the company. There are advantages for risk facilitators who are internal consultants: They know the culture of the organisation. They know what works and they're likely to be well aware of common issues. The disadvantage though, is that it can be easy to become caught up in internal politics. It can be difficult to remain as neutral as someone external.

Later, Penny left Mars to become an external consultant. That's another place where you can find risk facilitators. External consultants give you several advantages. They are more neutral than internal consultants. They specialise in risk and have lots of experience. (It's rare, though, for consultants to combine expertise in risk with the practical experience and skills in facilitation. This is why we have written this book to share our skills and experience across both areas.)

External experts with the right skills will have a wide view across different companies so they can see how you're doing in comparison to other companies. They can ask the 'dumb' questions that people inside the organisation would find difficult to ask. Of course, 'dumb' questions in reality may be clever questions and very helpful. External consultants are outside of the politics of the organisation in many respects.

What are some of the disadvantages of using external experts? Well, they may not know your organisational culture. They certainly won't have had the time that an internal consultant has had to pick up the culture and learn to work with it. They are also likely to cost more in the short term, so any additional expense upfront will need to be justified.

Here are two stories to show how effective risk facilitators can be inside organisations. Vivien and Anna's stories highlight different aspects of how to make risk management work.

VIVIEN'S STORY

HISTORY

Vivien works in risk within a major pharmaceutical company. A few years ago, the company had an electronic tool that was used to capture and track risks. To quote Vivien, 'The very nature of the tool killed energy and creativity.' The electronic tool needed a team of full-time experts whose sole job was to make sure that the tool was being used correctly and risks were added to it. However, these experts were rather out of touch with the main business. Managers would be trained on the tool but not in how to facilitate risk. They were expected to enter data into the tool as part of their job. Risk management wasn't really alive. The tool wasn't being used on an ongoing basis. People felt that they had to put data into the tool and once that was done, the job was done. But it wasn't.

THINGS START TO CHANGE

Since Vivien became involved, there have been many changes. Now both the purpose and objectives of risk management are very clear and there are formal criteria for what should be included. The old electronic tool has gone and has been replaced with simple templates. Risk is not just a focus for the risk team, but is part of the role of all managers. Instead of a specialist risk team, there is a whole network of risk people who have been trained in facilitation as well as risk. These risk facilitators ensure the 'process' works well, challenging facts and bringing energy to the risk management process.

Each category of risk has a global risk owner, who oversees that category as part of their role. The 'owners' ensure that risk is monitored and that appropriate actions are progressed. They are based in different business functions. The risk facilitators meet – normally virtually – to develop a central risk picture from across the business. Vivien provides ideas and risk themes to support their work. They run risk workshops to inspire the rest of the organisation.

The key thing about this change was to change the culture of the organisation, from turning a handle on a risk 'sausage machine' to keeping risk management alive.

THE RESULTS

How does risk management work now? Key performance indicators for risk are in place and reported against with information feeding up to the most senior levels of the organisation from different parts of the organisation globally. The board has a clear and comprehensive risk picture that is built up from reports from around the world. There is a network of people involved. There is an ongoing process, a very simple process, but it does enable people's buy-in and engagement. It keeps people accountable for their actions. The whole process is pragmatic and focuses on action rather than dictating precise steps to follow. Workshops are a key part, helping to embed risk into people's roles and responsibilities. The major risks to the organisation are updated quarterly, with an annual major refresh.

LESSONS FROM VIVIEN ON HOW TO MAKE RISK MANAGEMENT WORK

It's very easy when facilitating risk management to be unclear about what you're doing and why. This tends to leave people drowning in the detail. Everyone involved needs to know where their roles and responsibilities begin and end.

Vivien suggests that we should be really clear about who is accountable for each risk: 'Make sure there is ownership. When risks overlap areas, you'll need to choose whether to duplicate the ownership or to align and dovetail the ownership.'

Vivien feels that many organisations go straight to using a tool, especially when they have a lot of information. While tools can be helpful, she advises against using them at the very first stage.

The culture of the organisation is key to success. To make risk management work, you need people who are committed to identifying and responding to risk, not those who will only give lip service. You don't want 'handle-turners' to use the sausage machine metaphor again. Risk should be an integrated part of strategic and business performance planning.

Vivien told me more about the role of the risk facilitator, which has been so successful in her organisation. The risk facilitator needs to have creative skills, especially when it comes to working with groups. They need to be aware of a range of facilitation methods and be able to use those methods effectively. They need to be able to work both in a detailed way and at a big picture/high level to communicate better with the senior managers. The risk facilitator has to be able to challenge people at all levels of the organisation in order to be effective. This is crucial to success. Many people will portray issues as risks or try to avoid action. The risk facilitator needs to see connections between different things, to be able to spot risks that exacerbate each other across areas. While they might not manage projects as such, they'll find project management skills such as action tracking and following up to be very helpful. When working with senior people, their personal reputation and credibility is especially important as they need to be trusted. It's important too that risk facilitators understand the players and the politics involved.

Vivien was able to do all of these things herself and inspire others, which ultimately led to her success.

ANNA'S STORY

HISTORY

Anna works for a large IT company in a programme management office (PMO). The company has a very long-standing and well-developed risk management process that is thought through, properly documented and supported by a sophisticated tool. If you asked people in the organisation, they would say that risk management was very important: 'Just look at our process and tool!' In reality, there was mass 'lip-service' and the  extent and quality of implementation was very poor. Anna believed in the process and was frustrated with the response from her project manager, programme manager and senior management colleagues. What could she do to unlock the potential of the process?

THINGS START TO CHANGE

Anna runs a monthly risk governance meeting. The key people used either to attend reluctantly or not at all. The meeting process was well established and formulaic, with a detailed review of each project and the risks and risk responses within it. Anna decided to change this and to facilitate the next meeting in a different way. She circulated the information in advance (as usual) but asked each person to prepare a two-minute summary of what they were most worried about with their work at the current time. They were not constrained by reading the risks from the register. Rather they were encouraged to offer their personal summary of what was most risky and why about the work. The energy in the room was greatly improved in that meeting, and new risks were identified and new perspectives gained. The next month the same happened. It only took three to four months for the meetings to be transformed into interesting discussions that all the key people attended without exception. Anna was able to challenge more and facilitate discussions that just did not happen in the past.

RESULTS

The real test came when Anna was away from work with an illness for three months. On her return she was delighted to see that the process had continued during her absence. Without her, people were regularly identifying, prioritising and managing risks. Governance was effective in communicating shared risky areas, and escalating those risks that needed senior management action. Anna's senior manager commented, 'The difference between Anna and other risk specialists is that she listens to us, understands what we are saying, and doesn't beat us up with the minutiae of the process. We trust her to add value to any of our management meetings.' Anna said, 'I learned to let some things go, but I asked lots of questions so I understood the situation, then I could make the information fit into the official process back at my desk later. That way all the arguments about the process stopping the work getting done ended.'

LESSONS FROM ANNA ON HOW TO MAKE RISK MANAGEMENT WORK

Anna found a way to step out of the role of policeman, and into the role of facilitator. She didn't abandon her strong beliefs in the process itself. Nevertheless she did abandon trying to get the managers in her area to share her enthusiasm and belief. Instead she focused on what was on their minds, and took the detailed work of complying with the process through quality outputs away from them. Over time, they learned to do a good job themselves. This was a major step forward.

THE DEVELOPMENT PATH FOR RISK FACILITATORS

If you want to develop as a risk facilitator, how can you do this? How can you help your organisation develop an effective risk management culture?

1. ADVICE FOR INDIVIDUAL RISK FACILITATORS

How can you develop as a risk facilitator? Have a go in a small way at first, then get some support once you understand risk management as laid out in Chapter 2. Many people learn how to work with groups through years of experience. However we've found the *quickest* way to develop the specific skills of a risk facilitator is through a mixture of both training and support from risk facilitation experts *at the same time* as putting them into practice in the workplace. You can find out more about workshops to support you further, as well as assessing your skills as a risk facilitator, at www.facilitatingrisk.com.

To stretch your skills beyond your comfort zone, we suggest that you co-facilitate with somebody else who is more experienced than you. That way you can build up your experience. Later, you will be able to facilitate on your own at that level. Build up to larger groups, more diverse groups, and groups where the stakes are higher, the risks are larger and/or the people are more senior. Use the later chapters of this book for ideas you can try.

It's well worth working with others as you develop. Ruth and Penny recently worked with a team of three risk specialists within an organisation, to help them develop their skills as facilitators of the risk management process. They not only share ideas and support each other, but facilitate sessions together to build their skills and confidence.

We would strongly advise that individual risk facilitators find others to support them through their development process.

2. ADVICE FOR ORGANISATIONS

The development path for organisations is less clear.

How can you start to develop an organisation's approach? The first step is to make sure that people understand the value of the risk facilitator. Often administrators, risk coordinators or even people who handle the tools, are given the role, as opposed to skilled risk facilitators. The difference that skilled facilitators make is clear from Vivien and Anna's stories.

A key step is to define the role of the risk facilitator formally, in a job description or 'person specification' that people can be selected against. Once the role is accepted as necessary by senior leaders, others begin to accept that facilitation of risk management is crucial.

SUMMARY

Some key pointers for risk facilitators are:

1. They have a range of special skills.

2. They need to manage both the faciliation and the risk management process, but stay out of the content. They are vegetarian!

3. You can find them almost anywhere within organisations, as risk facilitation is a role and not a job.

4. They can develop their skills as individuals; we've shown a range of competencies to focus on and how.

5. A supportive organisational culture is required.

6. They can make a big difference.

With Vivien and Anna's stories, you can see how these play out in real life. In the next chapter, we'll look at how you can facilitate the risk process in different organisational settings and *contexts*.

(4) Facilitating the Risk Management Process

So far, we've explored the principles of risk management in Chapter 2 and looked at the role of the facilitator in Chapter 3. Now we put both together to cover how you can facilitate the risk management process.

Remember the hamburger model from the previous chapter? Great facilitators stay vegetarian: they don't get involved with the 'meat' that represents the actual risks. But risk facilitators do need to have the lettuce and tomato as well as the bun – they are responsible for making it easy for the group to implement really effective risk management. To do that they need to be well versed in risk management principles, tools and techniques, as well as being able to demonstrate all the qualities of a great facilitator.

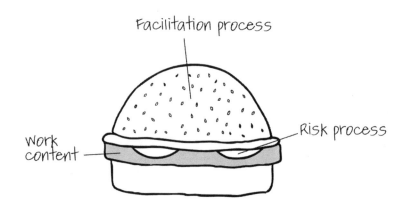

Facilitation process

Risk process

work content

NOT JUST WORKSHOPS

Many people will associate a risk facilitator with 'risk workshops'. The term 'risk workshop' is typically used to describe a situation where a group of people come together, either face-to-face or virtually to work through part of the risk management process. Facilitating workshops is a crucial part of the work – but not the only part.

The whole of the risk management process, from understanding objectives and tolerances through to monitoring and control, can be facilitated with great effect.

Great risk facilitators know how to engage the team and achieve the right balance between work done *'in'* workshops, and work done *'out'* of workshops. The right balance means only using workshops for work that requires creativity, collaboration, commitment, or for surfacing and dealing with conflict. It is better to do the work that requires detailed analysis in another way. Many people have told both Ruth and Penny that their experience of risk workshops is often dull and boring. However, we also know from feedback that workshops *can* be inspirational sessions that really get the team thinking and working together on risk. They can kick-start a focus on risk management that endures.

So, how can we all design our risk facilitation to inspire people, rather than put them to sleep? From our experience, there are three general 'rules'. These three rules are explained, followed by some examples of tried and tested ways to get the work done.

GENERAL RULES FOR RISK FACILITATION

ENGAGE THE RIGHT PEOPLE AT THE RIGHT TIME

It's really important that you learn who the stakeholders are and where those stakeholders are coming from in terms of objectives, power, interest and attitude. This will start with your 'client' for the work. If a formal stakeholder analysis exists, get hold of it and verify the information. If not, ask lots of questions and make sure you have a good understanding of who is involved and what their perspectives on risk are likely to be before you start to engage them. You also need to know some other practical things about stakeholders, such as where they're located, their national cultural background, their past experience of risk management, whether they have funding to travel, and so on. The more you know at the start, the easier it will be as you progress.

ENERGISE, AND KEEP THE ENERGY

Doing risk management well is detailed and often difficult work. This means it can so easily become laborious and frustrating. As facilitator, you need to take responsibility for helping the team find as well as maintain focus and energy. Doing this, in turn,  can take a lot of your energy as you work on creating the right group dynamic as well as keeping focused enough to be able to challenge. Our own experience is that helping the group to become positively energised and to keep that energy becomes much easier the more experienced you become with implementing the risk management process. Once these skills become second nature to you, it will free you up to focus on the group rather than the process, and the different ways to keep the group engaged and participating.

CHALLENGE, BUT STAY VEGETARIAN

This can be tricky. Your quest as a risk facilitator is to uphold the quality of the risk management process. You need to tease out risks from issues, challenge pre-conceived views, be able to see if there is systematic bias emerging, or offer alternative strategies when response planning. Your challenge is to refrain from offering your own perceptions of the nature and extent of risks, or your opinions about priorities and responses. *The group own the risks.* You are there simply to ease the process to define and manage those risks. So keep your challenges vegetarian and things should be OK.

WHAT TO DO, AND WAYS TO DO IT

In this section we break the risk management process down into separate steps, highlight the questions that each step of the process must answer, and the outputs that are needed. We also outline some different ways that we have facilitated each step of the process ourselves. These are offered as tried and tested examples. There will, of course, be many other ways to achieve successful outcomes.

GOVERNANCE OF THE RISK MANAGEMENT PROCESS

Governance must underpin all the process steps. What does this mean? In this context, governance simply means that the senior leaders of the organisation must put in place arrangements to monitor progress, to escalate or delegate decisions to the right level of management, and to provide a decision-making regime that gets best use from the risk management process. By doing this, senior leaders begin to show their support for risk management.

In the most successful organisations, senior leaders provide a supportive culture. Here the nature of uncertainty and risk are understood, and the management of uncertainties that matter most is measurably efficient *and* effective.

STEP 1: INITIATING RISK MANAGEMENT, OR 'HOW MUCH RISK CAN WE TOLERATE?'

Questions to be answered	Outputs
• Who are the stakeholders? • What are their objectives? • How will these be measured? • Who will judge? • Which objectives take (relative) priority when things get tough? • How much risk to these objectives are you prepared to tolerate? • What process will you use to manage the risks to objectives?	SMART (specific, measurable, agreed, realistic and timed) statements of objectives in priority order, with defined impact scales and risk tolerances for each objective. Risk management plan, including a stakeholder analysis and engagement plan, and defined and agreed probability and impact scales.

Tried and tested tips

- If it is possible to get the key people together easily, then using a couple of hours in a face-to-face workshop can be a really effective way to answer the questions. Take the follow-up work off-line: tidying the input and presenting back SMART statements of objectives along with a draft risk management plan.

- If people are spread out geographically, but know one-another and the work to be done, you can use a virtual meeting with a shared screen where you can share information in real time. As before, tidy the input and present back SMART statements of objectives along with a draft risk management plan off-line.

- If people are geographically spread out and don't know one-another well, you can work with one or two senior people to prepare a draft set of objectives and risk management plan. After this you can take the time to share this with the other stakeholders in one-to-one telephone calls, inviting them to share any different perspectives they have. When you have verified (or otherwise) the draft objectives and plan, you can then decide how to progress. When there are different perspectives – and there usually are – you can bring people together to resolve any differences at the start of the next stage.

STEP 2: IDENTIFYING AND DESCRIBING INDIVIDUAL RISKS OR 'WHAT'S RISKY AND WHY?'

Questions to be answered	Outputs
• What are the potential opportunities – things that might occur that would improve the achievement of objectives? • What are the potential problems, things that might occur that would harm the achievement of objectives? • Who is the best owner for each risk?	List of risks, described well, separating causes, from risk events from effects (as described in Chapter 2).

This is work that requires:

• creativity, to open up the mind to what may occur; and

• detailed work – to explore the relationships between causes, risk events and effects and to write clear risk descriptions.

Tried and tested tips

• If you can get the group together face-to-face and you have good experience in facilitating risk management, you may well be able to facilitate the creative and detailed aspects of this step together, that is, by taking the output from the group and turning it into clear and complete descriptions during the workshop. Ruth has done this with groups of more than 20 people and captured the risk descriptions on flipcharts. These were pasted up around the room. An alternative to this is to capture the output straight into a table of risks on a laptop projected onto a wall. This output will be ready to send out electronically immediately after the workshop.

- If you can get the group together face-to-face but have less time together, or are less experienced, it can be more useful to facilitate a creative session with the group first, capturing the outputs in any way you wish. Then take them off-line to create detailed risk descriptions for the risk register. Share this work with the group to validate and/or change the draft descriptions at a later time.

- If it is difficult to get the group together face-to-face, try using a remote brainstorming technique to get each individual to identify risks, and then share the output with the whole group to continue the creative process. Modern technology has enabled a number of innovative solutions to this sort of task. You, as facilitator, can take time during this process to make sure causes, risk events and effects are clearly articulated so that the output is clear and everyone agrees with it.

Potential problems and potential opportunities

Whatever approach you use for risk identification, we have found that some experienced groups are able to deal with the identification of potential opportunities and potential problems in the same process. In contrast, less experienced groups often struggle with this. Our experience is that it is useful to focus on identifying potential opportunities *first*. When no more can be identified, then move to the threats. One of our colleagues also makes great use of physical prompts such as issuing 'rose-tinted spectacles' to people to help them think positively, or by putting the ideas behind De Bono's *Six Thinking Hats*, for example the yellow hat for optimism, to great use. Sensing when such prompts can help a group progress is a key skill of a successful facilitator.

STEP 3: PRIORITISING INDIVIDUAL RISKS OR 'HOW MUCH DOES EACH RISK MATTER?'

Questions to be answered	Outputs
• How would the identified risks impact on objectives if they occurred? • What is the chance that each risk would have that impact on objectives?	Register of unmanaged risks populated, prioritised, challenged and communicated to relevant stakeholders.

This is the step in the process that is the most subjective and the most open to human bias. It's the step that can really sap energy if the group feel that their efforts are not leading to good outcomes. Facilitators can make a huge difference here. In addition to the well-described risks from the previous step, you need to have the probability and impact scales already agreed. Remember that these scales articulate what matters most and how much risk can be tolerated.

Tried and tested tips

- If you decide to facilitate this step of the process in a face-to-face workshop, the key thing is to keep the assessment as objective as possible, while keeping everyone involved. We strongly advise *not* to have the whole group of people assessing probability and impact together. This takes too long and is one sure way of supporting the reputation of risk management of being tedious and dull! It doesn't have to be like this.

- One idea is to separate the assessment of impact from the assessment of probability. For example, if risks are written on flip-charts pasted around the room, you can have the group on their feet, starting at different places and walking around. They can add their assessment of impact beside each risk and note differences in opinion from other group members with arrows (up or down from the first assessment). The process can then be repeated for the assessment of probability. To make this work well, especially with an inexperienced group, you need clear rules for framing the questions to be answered. Agree these and put them on the wall.

The questions that this step of the process must answer are:

- If this risk occurred, how big would the impact be? (As per the defined impact scales.)

And

- What is the chance that this risk might occur? (As per the defined probability scales.)

Another technique in a workshop setting is to break up the group into smaller teams, with each team considering a proportion of the defined risks. The output from each smaller team can then be consolidated in a visual way and challenged by the other teams afterwards. At this stage any systematic bias can be challenged and dealt with. If you are using this technique, it's good to plan in some time for you as facilitator to consolidate the output. Ruth's experience facilitating risk workshops is that she always plans for a consolidating task to do over lunchtime in order to keep the process moving. (You get used to taking your food and drink when the group is working!) An alternative, of course, is to work on prioritising risks in an afternoon session, consolidate overnight then challenge the following morning.

Although it would be typical for this step to be done in a face-to-face workshop, we could argue that this is not actually the best way. A remote technique is much better at getting each individual stakeholder's perspective in the first instance. The output can then be pulled together by the facilitator remotely and shared – either virtually again, or better still at the start of a group workshop.

Think again how workshops are used

In our experience, most groups seem to use workshops to facilitate every step of the process up to this point, that is to set objectives and the scales for prioritisation, to identify and describe risks and to prioritise them. After this the group is typically out of time, or out of energy to do more. For this reason we would encourage everyone to think about doing the work up to this point in the process differently. For example using separate short workshops if the geography allows, or using virtual techniques to get to the point where all stakeholders have had their input on the risks and their priority. After this you can bring the group together for challenge, consolidation and response planning. Varying the way you achieve the outcomes of this step of the process also prevents stagnation and boredom.

STEP 4: ASSESSING OVERALL RISKINESS, OR 'HOW RISKY IS THIS SITUATION?'

Questions to be answered	Outputs
• Which risks are mutually exclusive? • Which risks are correlated? • What is the combined impact of all risks on objectives?	Visualisation of the combined risk impact on objectives. *Note: this can be done qualitatively or quantitatively depending on the needs of the organisation.*

This step of the process is often missed out which then leaves a big gap in the value of the risk management process. An overall map of the risks to objectives is a useful way to support assessment of the overall riskiness of the situation. Mutually exclusive risks must be identified, so, if risk A occurs, risk B cannot. Similarly, correlated risks must be identified, so, if risk C occurs then risk D must also.

Tried and tested tips

• This step works best with a small number of people, ideally just the risk owners, coming together on a face-to-face basis to create the overall map of risks. If it's not possible to get the right people physically together, the same effect can be created by the facilitator carrying out a series of interviews then piecing together the overall picture. However, this is more difficult to do well and takes a lot more time. The facilitator must ensure there is understanding of how each of the risks relate to each other as this is a necessary first step for subsequent qualitative, or quantitative analysis.

- Most organisations visualise the complete set of risks in a situation on some sort of grid, typically called a probability/impact grid, a risk assessment matrix, or a heat map. The beauty of such visualisations is that they can be both created, and kept up to date easily. There are many different ways of creating such visualisations. We strongly recommend using a method where you can clearly visualise both potential problems and potential opportunities. Some organisations do not do any further analysis of the combined impact of all risks on objectives.

- If your organisation uses a more sophisticated, quantitative technique, building probabilistic models and analysing these statistically, then our top tips for getting quality output are as follows. First, be sure that the 'right' stakeholders are involved – those with relevant experience and those who know what historical data is relevant and available. Second, be sure that the team has at least one member who understands the statistics involved and can help the team avoid building anomalies into the model. The effect of the central limit theorem or nodal bias can cause particular problems – someone in the team must understand how to overcome such problems. Third, make sure there is a transparent link between the risk register and the risk model, that is, that the range estimates and judgements of probability have taken into account the risks that have been identified. Finally, have the model and the outputs from the simulations had a 'sanity check' by challenging the underlying assumptions of the model?

STEP 5: RESPONDING TO RISKS, OR 'WHAT ACTION SHALL WE TAKE?'

Questions to be answered	Outputs
• Can the risks be tolerated and left unmanaged? • If not, what is the response to each risk that gives best value for money/effort? • Who will do what to manage the risk? • What risk is expected to remain if response plans are effective? (residual risk) • What other risks might be caused by the response plan? (secondary risks)	Updated risk register to include response plans and expected residual risk, and identification of any secondary risks. Updated plans.

Chapter 2 outlined the options open to risk owners: take the risk, prepare a plan B, treat the risk, share (not transfer) the risk or make it certain. Most typically this work is not done in face-to-face meetings or workshops because:

• the workshop has been used for earlier stages in the process and the team have run out of time and/or steam; and/or

• the work of response planning is delegated to risk owners.

This can be the start of the potential decline in attention given to risk management; the slide from the energised workshop to the stagnant process. What can be done differently?

Tried and tested tips

• There are big benefits in using the group who assessed the overall riskiness of the work in the previous step staying together to plan responses. They can then share their output with the wider group of stakeholders at a later stage. The benefits of this approach arise because the group is concentrating not just on individual risks, but the combined effect of risks to objectives. Keeping this concentration ensures responses focused on the defined risk tolerance for the work and a sense of value, that is, is the action you take to respond to a risk worth it?

- In particularly complex, risky situations, you could consider using what is known as a scenario planning technique. Scenario planning is completely reliant on great facilitation. Originally a strategic planning technique, it can be used to get groups of people to envisage possible alternative futures, and then to plan what actions are needed to secure the desired future outcome. Ruth has used this technique with groups who knew what they wanted to achieve, but where the route to achieving that was complex because of many competing threats and opportunities. Creating a setting where people can tell stories and draw visual depictions of action plans to respond to the risks is a key part of making scenario planning work well.

- Another option is to invite different 'experts' to share their experiences and suggest response options. People who are not stakeholders for the work, but who have experience of doing similar things are ideal contributors. They are not emotionally attached to the work and achievement of objectives and can often cut through bias by challenging perspectives. In our experience, the facilitator's job in such a situation is to get the best out of the visitors while at the same time ensuring that the team can 'hear' the advice. It goes without saying that this option requires a setting where people are open and willing to consider different perspectives.

- Ultimately, response plans need to be 'worth it', that is, the investment in the response plan can be justified in terms of the reduction in residual risk. We have found that facilitators can be of great worth here by providing challenge to make sure that the investment in risk management is demonstrably beneficial.

STEP 6: KEEPING THE PROCESS ALIVE, OR 'WHAT'S THE CURRENT STATUS?'

Questions to be answered	Outputs
• What has changed since the last review?	Updated risk register.

Tried and tested tips

You may recall from both Vivien and Anna's stories in Chapter 3 that they had found a way of keeping the process alive. Unfortunately, this is rare.

If the rest of the process has gone well, the challenge at this stage is how to track and manage a large number of well-described and assessed risks.

This is a question posed by one of our clients:

> *I am hoping you will be able to offer some advice on conducting risk review meetings and using the time effectively. We recently carried out a risk facilitation session with the senior management team to generate a new risk register. We used a lot of the interactive techniques you taught us and the response was excellent.*

One of the problems, however, is that we now have a huge number of risks to manage! We have two registers – one for the business that contains mainly reputation, health and safety, and people risks. We have 63 risks on this risk register and reviews take place quarterly. The second register is the 'Programme' register that has 156 risks and contains commercial, delivery and programme delivery risks. Reviews take place monthly. Both registers have a good mix of threats and opportunities.

***How do we review these effectively?** Do we need to focus attention only on the top priority risks? I did this at the last programme review and it took 3 hours! We just about managed this, but it was a painful and slow process, and I was conscious of 130 others that we didn't even touch on. After the meeting I sent out a filtered version to the owners of lower priority risks that we didn't get round to reviewing and only 1 of the 10 got back to me. The only other thing I could do is set up further 1:1's, but some owners have 20+ risks on the register and are unlikely to commit to another meeting every month on the back of the group 3-hour meeting. This is very time consuming for me as well, but I'm worried that after all the good work that has gone in to identifying all these risks nothing will change because nobody is reviewing them!*

I know it's difficult and it's the behaviours that need to change but any suggestions or tips you have on how I could improve on this would be much appreciated.

Our response was as follows:

First – the very worst outcome here is that the list of risks are seen as *your* risks and the review process as *your* review. This can result in the managers involved feeling it's a chore and they're doing you a favour.

Second – I worry about only reviewing the top risks (that is, the most likely, biggest impact). It is critical to keep an eye on low probability/high impact risks as a minimum as these are often the ones that become real issues.

Some ideas to try are:

- You could devise a process where each risk owner comes to the review with a short exception report about their risks, that is, which ones have been worked on, which ones they're most worried about (threats), or enthusiastic about (opportunities), ones where, in their view, the priority has changed since last time, and, most importantly, the ones where they need help to manage them from elsewhere. I'm not sure how many risk owners there are but if everyone had a ten-minute slot this would be doable. Everyone would learn from listening to their colleagues, for example, you could start to get information about common responses/solutions. You could even capture the content and then update the risk register off-line. They could present their information any way they liked, as long as it covered the ground.

- Tell them that you want to make the face-to-face time you have together as rich as possible – so ask people to give you an update off-line before the meeting (using the same format as described above. You can then bring the risks that are most noteworthy to the meeting for discussion. This way the meeting doesn't get bogged down in boring reporting. Needless to say, this relies on an investment in time ahead of the meeting, but it would have a pay-off in terms of the actual quality of the meeting process and output.

- If you can't split the risk register by risk owner, you could divide it by line manager, or by risk 'type', that is commercial, delivery, programme delivery and so on. However with this suggestion it may be more difficult to get one person to take ownership of the feedback provided.

- To show this visually, you could have a traffic light system, along the following lines:

Red: a concern (either because risk is not being managed, it hasn't been reviewed for three months or more, or it doesn't have an agreed response);

Amber: a minor concern (not managed, hasn't been reviewed for two months, or is out of date in some way); and

Green: only achieved if the risk has been reviewed in the last month and has an agreed response plan that is under control (even if the response is simply to accept and monitor).

- It's also really important to remain focused on the overall objectives for the work and the amount of risk that the organisation is prepared to take. Our experience is that keeping a focus on overall riskiness puts the detailed work of reviewing individual risks in context.

SUMMARY

This chapter had two objectives. The first was to outline a practical and usable risk management process, by outlining the key steps of the process and the questions that need to be answered by each step. The second was to share some of our experiences of how to facilitate the risk management process in a way that:

- engages the right people at the right time;

- uses approaches that energise people and keep the energy throughout; and

- focuses on the role of the facilitator as a risk process expert, but also as a vegetarian who stays out of the 'meat' of the situation, empowering the group to be accountable for the process outputs.

The tried and tested approaches in this chapter work for us and should provide enough guidance for you to try different approaches, from which you can develop your own.

It is important to remember that an effective risk facilitator cannot make risk management work all on their own. The organisation will need governance that supports risk management and provides a decision-making regime that can make good decisions in risky and important situations.

Workshops are a part of the solution, where they are designed to achieve a specific purpose. The next chapter will go into more details of how to plan and deliver successful risk workshops.

REFERENCES

De Bono, E. (2000) *Six Thinking Hats*, London: Penguin.

⑤ Risk Workshops

Workshops are just part of the risk process, but they're a very important part, which we'll cover in this chapter.

Why are workshops so important? They are where representatives of different areas get together. In a workshop, you are able to generate ideas as a group, build consensus and agreement, and come up with decisions. Often, you can sort out differences  and misunderstandings immediately. If you design your process well, you can build shared ownership of outcomes. In workshops, people can be listened to, feel heard by others and give voice to concerns. When people have the opportunity to work together on outputs, workshops can be so much more than dumping grounds of all of the risks that people could dream up individually. In a workshop, there's a chance to deal with different perceptions of what is risky and why. You can also challenge any bias that can so easily occur, such as 'groupthink' or other sources of bias as covered in Appendix A in Chapter 2. All of these workshop benefits will only come with good facilitation.

Workshops can work very well as part of the process. But they're *not* the whole process. Many people try to do everything as a workshop, whereas a mixture of larger workshops, small sub-groups and one-to-one work is more likely to be successful. See Chapter 4 for our recommendations on how to create the right mix.

Workshops give us an opportunity to do something different and creative, to break out of what has been a formulaic way of dealing with risk in many organisations.

Here's an example of a successful, half-day risk workshop that is still having an impact:

> *Tony, who works in local government in Wales, recalled a risk identification workshop for the regeneration of Cardiff Harbour. It lasted half a day but is still having a positive impact ten years later.*
>
> *He talked through how they got it right. 'We brought in external facilitators and had a good range of stakeholders present. We came up with a huge range of risks, from World War II unexploded bombs to alien invasion!' Tony went on to explain that alien invasion didn't mean little green men from Mars, but rather the possibility of the ecosystem in a new freshwater lake getting out of balance. This could mean plagues of midges and other small insects, which would spoil the new environment for local people and visitors,*

including wedding guests nearby. Tony described how they set aside funding, which allowed them to reduce this risk by stocking the lake with fish and injecting insecticide into mud to kill off midge larvae. A few years later, the risk became an issue (the risk actually occurred) and further measures were needed.

Now, Cardiff Bay has been visited by teams from as far afield as Venice, Korea and the USA as a case study for controlling alien invasion. Tony has continued to be committed to risk. He's found the way to keep risk alive in his authority. 'With the right people, who all care about what we're doing, it'll stay on the agenda!'

That workshop certainly worked for Tony. How can you make yours as successful?

Let's look at risk workshops in three parts:

1. The work you do beforehand to prepare for a workshop.

2. Running the workshop itself.

3. How you can get actions completed after the workshop is over.

PREPARING FOR A WORKSHOP

First of all, agree the objectives of this particular workshop with your senior manager and be clear on the benefits of doing this work together. Remember that the workshop is just one part of a bigger process. It helps to explain a clear vision of what's important and why, as well as the benefits of doing this workshop.

Are there any issues, conflicts or politics that you should know about which could affect this workshop? These are likely to be sources of risk too.

The key question to answer for workshops is: *'What is the point?'* What is the purpose of running this particular workshop at this time? Make sure that's really clear and stated in any invitation.

WHO SHOULD BE THERE AND FOR WHICH PARTS OF THIS WORKSHOP?

Not everybody needs to be there for the whole time. You might want some specialists to come in just for a small part of the session. How many people should be there? It's often good to get representatives of different areas concerned and you'll find guidelines for who should take part in a variety of types of workshop in Chapter 4. Remember too that workshops become less efficient with large numbers. Think through who you need to make this part of the process work, and make sure you have people from the right levels within your organisation, as well as the right number.

WHAT ROLES ARE NEEDED FOR AN EFFECTIVE WORKSHOP?

There are at least three:

1. There's the *risk facilitator*, who facilitates the meeting. As such, their role is to stay out of the details of the content. They need to be able to challenge people about their perception of risks.

 2. *Timekeeper:* It helps to appoint someone else to keep an eye on how much time is left and how you're progressing through the agenda. Their role is to keep you on track.

3. *A recorder (or scribe)* can capture the output, including decisions and actions, so that they can be shared immediately afterwards.

WHAT ABOUT THE TIMING OF THE WORKSHOP?

How long should the workshop last? There is always a balance to strike between maintaining energy, and making maximum use of the time that people can be together. There are some creative options you can use to get this balance right. Chapter 4 has much more to say on this, including some tips on how many risk workshops may be needed to cover the whole risk management process.

WHAT ARE THE OBJECTIVES?

What do you want to have achieved by the end of your risk workshop?

IS THERE ANY PRELIMINARY WORK THAT SHOULD BE DONE?

As the facilitator you will want to prepare carefully. Do you have enough resources available, including an appropriate room or an effective virtual meeting tool? Have you thought about lessons that have been learned on similar workshops in the past? For each particular workshop, you can check for the inputs you'll need from previous parts of the process, as shown in Chapter 4.

HOW WELL DO PEOPLE COMING TO THIS WORKSHOP UNDERSTAND RISK?

Their understanding may be very basic. Often people will require a quick reminder of the basics as laid out in Chapter 2.

WHAT ABOUT THE DIVERSITY OF THE GROUP?

Do you need to plan carefully in this area? For example, if you have somebody who is known to be very loud and you have others who are likely to be very quiet, how will you handle that? What about people at differing levels of seniority within the organisation? If you have a mixture of hierarchies in the room, it's important not to ignore this as it will affect the dynamics in the room. One option is to form small, mixed groups that then feed back to the whole workshop. Another option is to use some forms of anonymous input.

What about the mixture of professionals? For example, engineers and marketing specialists often behave quite differently in workshops. What about cross-cultural issues? These can be as much between organisations as well as between people from different countries. There are many things that influence people's attitude to specific risks. Thinking how you will deal with diversity in advance will help you prepare for a great workshop.

WHAT ABOUT HIDDEN AGENDAS?

Are there likely to be any? Plan to find these out beforehand to uncover other aspects of politics which could affect your workshop. If you're fairly new to risk facilitation, check with somebody experienced to make sure that nothing has been missed.

There is one element of workshops that is usually left out, although its inclusion makes a big difference. This is to set *very clear rules*, or ways of working, and agree them at the start of the workshop. These are sometimes called ground rules. They give you a chance to anticipate problems and address them up front before the problems occur. By anticipating problems in this way, the risk facilitator has much more chance of a successful workshop. Some examples of ground rules include:

1. How people will use mobiles and laptops. A common rule here is to keep mobiles on silent and laptops closed during the workshop sessions, but not breaks.

2. Respecting confidentiality. Which aspects of the workshop need to be kept secret and why? You might agree to allow all information to be shared, but keep the name of the contributor anonymous, as an example.

3. One tip that I find very useful is to write down 'spellling dusn't mattter.' It normally raises a laugh and takes the pressure off anybody who is writing in public.

THINK ABOUT HOW ACTIONS WILL BE RECORDED ACCURATELY DURING THE WORKSHOP

How are you going to keep track of them? Can the scribe write them out? If somebody is going to type them into a computer, can you make them visible to everyone in real time? How are you going to make sure that everyone is clear on the next steps? How will you follow up to make sure actions are done after the workshop?

MAKE SURE YOU ISSUE AN INVITATION TO THE APPROPRIATE PEOPLE

Do this well in advance of the workshop. This should contain the purpose of the meeting, the objectives, the agenda, who is participating and include links to any preparatory information. Ensure that all the other resources are available for the day, from the meeting room to the materials you need.

WORKSHOP ENVIRONMENT

Where will you hold the workshop? How can you create the right atmosphere? Think of all five senses, and how you can create a good environment in terms of:

1. *Sight:* Natural light keeps people much more alert than fluorescent light, so avoid dark basement rooms. Make sure that everyone can see any shared material, such as

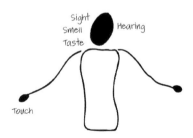

recorded risks and actions. Can you share these on-screen for remote participants?

2. *Sound:* The best background for effective work is a quiet and peaceful room away from traffic noise and free from loud air-conditioning. With virtual working, a clear audio-conferencing line is absolutely essential. Make sure everyone can hear all the contributions easily. People may need to mute their line when not speaking to ensure a clear line for all.

3. *Touch:* Are the chairs comfortable? Are the tables clean?

4. *Taste:* Have you provided some food to keep people going? Fresh fruit or nuts are more effective than biscuits and cakes as they avoid a sugar high and the subsequent crash.

5. *Smell:* Is the room stuffy after a previous meeting? Can you open the windows?

DURING THE WORKSHOP

We recommend that you have a plan for your risk workshop, with processes and resources in place from start to finish. However, facilitated workshops seldom run to plan! You have to be prepared to divert if your initial plan doesn't work quite as well as you had hoped. If you've prepared well, and have a range of options, then things are likely to run much more smoothly.

Before you begin, you might find it helpful to kick off your workshop with a senior sponsor or manager summarising why this particular workshop is important to your organisation.

At the start of a workshop, run through all the steps shown in Figure 5.1. If you've prepared carefully, and communicated carefully with everyone beforehand, this should just be a reprise for everyone. It provides the group with the opportunity to have their input and if necessary make changes.

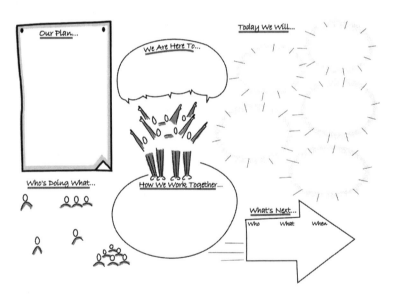

Figure 5.1   A summary of steps to start up any workshop (used with permission)

1. *We are here to:* What's the purpose of your workshop today? Once this is agreed, display it so that everyone can see it. This will help you keep on track.

2. *Today we will:* What do you want to achieve by the end; what are the objectives for the meeting?

3. *Our plan:* What is the agenda? What happens when?

4. *Who's doing what:* What are the roles and who will play them? Choose a timekeeper and a scribe at this point of the meeting if you haven't already done so.

5. *How we work together:* What are the ground rules? This step is very important to anticipate problems and to make it clear how the workshop will run.

6. *What's next:* Talk about how actions will be captured and followed up.

INTRODUCE RISK MANAGEMENT

Run through the key risk concepts needed for this particular workshop at the start, so that everyone is clear.

HOW DO YOU KEEP TO TIME?

The facilitator needs to strike a balance between the needs of some to go into detail and the time available. For example, in a workshop that is planning responses to previously identified and prioritised risks, you may need to intervene to stop too much discussion about lower priority risks. Our experience is that people can get carried away discussing risks they care much about, but which in the greater scheme of things don't warrant the air-time. These could be low probability/ low impact risks for example. The facilitator has a crucial role here to move the group along, while at the same time acknowledging the importance of the risk to the people involved. Here's an example:

> 'We've spent the last hour discussing risks in the Human Resources area. We have five other areas to cover today. Should we continue in HR and schedule a further workshop for tomorrow for the others, or should we move on now? What's your view?'

HOW DO YOU STAY CALM AS FACILITATOR?

Although it's critical for the process to have energy, the facilitator needs to find a way of remaining calm throughout. The very nature of workshops is that you cannot predict what will happen. To prevent unexpected situations getting to you, it's useful to have tactics for staying calm.

At the start, you might find it helpful to 'anchor' your mind to a successful workshop in the past. Remember that you don't always have to be busy doing or saying something. Often quiet thought, rather than a quick response, will stand you in good stead. You really need to be able to manage your own 'state' as a facilitator, staying centred and effective, even when things get tough.

One helpful way of doing this is to reflect back what you see happening in the group, rather than taking it upon yourself to 'fix' the group. Remember that the group owns the risks and the group owns the results. The facilitator doesn't. The group can decide what to do as a result. It takes the pressure off the risk facilitator. This technique has been important for Penny as she moved from working with small project groups to large international programmes of change.

WHAT DO YOU DO DURING THE WORKSHOP IF IT ALL GOES HORRIBLY WRONG?

Risk facilitators are often anxious about things going wrong in their sessions and wonder what they would do. Of course, things often don't go as planned. One obvious tactic if things take a turn for the worse is  to take a short break. This is often quite as much of a relief to the group, as to the facilitator. Often, a simple chat with people individually will put the workshop back on track. Try not to be 'in control and in charge' but facilitate the group to do their best. The biggest mistake you can make is to behave as if it's your workshop and you own the outputs. This isn't true, as it is the group's workshop and they own the outputs. It would be far better to acknowledge the issues and ask the group for their suggestions. If you are concerned about failure, read through Chapter 6 and make sure you've covered the potential pitfalls of risk workshops.

HOW ARE YOU GOING TO GATHER INPUT?

You might want to do use brainstorming. A crucial ground rule for gathering a large number of ideas in this way is to make sure that all contributions are constructive, rather than negative or critical. It's the facilitator's job to ensure this by challenging anyone who comes up with negative comments at this early stage. The group will be able to judge all the contributions once the creative part is over.

Another good way of gathering input is to encourage people to share lessons learned from previous work.

Use the fact that you will have more than one workshop. The time in-between workshops is ideal for the participants to go away and come back with thought-through ideas to the next step.

USE ANONYMOUS INPUT TO GOOD EFFECT

You can use anonymous ways of gathering input to get the widest possible range of ideas. This works especially when you have a wide range of people with different levels of power in the organisation, or when people prefer not to speak controversial ideas out loud. In a face-to-face meeting, you can ask people to write on Post-it™ notes and stick them up. In virtual meetings, use a tool or a third party to gather input from each participant in an anonymous way.

Another way of gathering risk ideas face-to-face is to cover a table with paper. Give everyone a set of pens of the same colour and ask them to stand around the table. Write the question in the centre. For example, 'What are all the risks that might happen to this project?' Ask everybody to write down everything that come to mind. Then get the group to move slowly around the table adding on further comments until they return to where they started. This is a very quick way to gather a large number of ideas from a group.

Figure 5.2 is an example used to gather issues people face in risk workshops as part of the research for Chapter 6 (thanks to the Association for Project Management Programme Management Specific Interest Group).

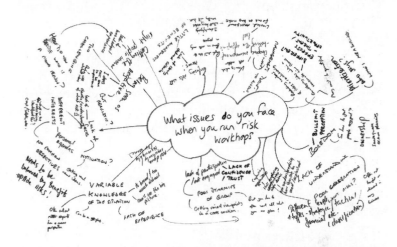

Figure 5.2   A group map built by APM members about the issues they face with risk workshops (used with permission)

Penny used the group mind-map technique where she only had 20 minutes for a workshop on a major programme. When she joined the programme, it had a mantra: 'We have a thousand ways to fail, but we proceed valiantly.' The first thing Penny did was to spend all 20 minutes running a risk identification workshop. You should have seen the relief on the faces of the people involved, as they realised that the risky areas had actually been identified and were going to be investigated. They wouldn't have to wake up in the middle of the night in cold sweats as they thought of yet more unidentified risks ever again!

VISIBLE INFORMATION

It can be very helpful for groups to see what they've been talking about. So how can you make the discussion visible to people? Penny uses techniques of recording words and pictures to make sure that all the ideas are visible to the whole group. An example of this might be each person writing down their own ideas on sticky notes and then presenting them in clusters on a wall. Alternatively, the risk facilitator or scribe can write down risks on a flipchart, board or shared screen as they are raised.

TEAM STAGES

It's good practice to make sure you are aware how teams form: the common stages that all teams go through. One way of understanding this is by using the Tuckman Team Development Model. This predicts four stages in turn:

1. *Forming*: where the team come together;

2. *Storming*: where people jostle for position;

3. *Norming:* where people begin to settle down into group 'norms'; and finally,

4. *Performing:* where the team work together effectively.

Knowing that these stages are going to happen, it makes sense to include introductions to help the team form and ground rules to help the team to 'norm'. Facilitators who know that 'storming' will come before 'norming' will expect some disagreements and want to resolve these to move on. For the team to really 'perform', the facilitator must help to create a productive atmosphere where people bring their energy to the task in hand.

It's helpful to be aware of a range of models, because different models have elements which work better in different situations and which highlight different aspects of team working. No model is completely right on its own in all situations. Another that we've used to good effect is the Drexler/Sibbet Team Performance Model. We particularly like this model as it makes it very clear that team performance depends on establishing good foundations for team working at the start of the workshop. It shows clearly how the team need to be clear on their purpose and to build trust *before* clarifying goals and gaining commitment. Only then does action follow, and possibly high performance. The model uses the analogy of a bouncing ball: the more effort put in upfront, the higher the ball will bounce.

CONFLICT

Be aware of conflict. In fact, you should expect it. Conflict just means that there are some disagreements, which mean that there are different perspectives. Use them, don't hide them. You get better decisions when there has been some element of this 'task' conflict.

However, you don't want to have personal relationship conflict or fights breaking out within your risk workshop (or even small nuclear explosions!). It's not usually a major problem, but if this does happen, you'll need to sort it out immediately. To do so, highlight what you see happening, rather than 'sweeping it under the carpet' and hoping it will go away. It won't. Refer people back to the ground rules that you set up at the start of the session and ask them to abide by the agreed rules. You may need to come up with some new ground rules as a group to deal with any issues. Consider calling a break and talking with the individuals concerned. Remember to stay neutral and to focus on what you can see and hear, rather than judgements and inferences. Another useful to tip is to 'be hard on the issue yet soft on the person'. Keep the group focused on the work issue at hand and not on personalities. If you know that relationship conflict is likely to arise, you'll need to prepare even more thoroughly than usual, carefully discussing issues with the people concerned. It may help to bring in an experienced facilitator, who will have experience and training in conflict management.

WORKING VIRTUALLY

Many people are called upon to run risk workshops virtually. This means that the group works together while they are separated geographically. These virtual meetings can work very well using conference call or video conferencing, with shared screens or a remote collaboration system. You'll need to spend even more time in preparation than in face-to-face meetings. It's also best to use a facilitator who is skilled at remote facilitation.

Try to keep your virtual workshops short (an hour is plenty). This means you may need to split each workshop into several remote sessions. Remember, too, that detailed information is best shared outside the workshop through e-mail or shared databases. As risk management can get very detailed, this helps to prevent people becoming overwhelmed during the workshop itself. (This tip also works for face-to-face workshops!)

It's even more of a challenge to keep people engaged and involved when your workshop is virtual. Ask people for their comments throughout the workshop to keep them involved. (Incidentally, it's a good idea to let people know that you'll be doing this at the start, so that there are no surprises.)

Another tip to help people connect is to provide a photo map: a map showing the geographic location of each person, along with their photo.

When working virtually it's important to build up the trust and commitment of each individual in the team. The key to this is to have one-to-one conversations outside of the risk workshops. If possible, hold the first workshop in a series face-to-face. This will help build the relationships that will sustain the group over the rest of the risk management process.

Vinit, a project manager based in the Middle East, told us his story of facilitating across several countries in Asia:

> 'When we held risk identification workshops, no one would speak up! What changed this was putting in a lot of time individually with people to build trust and to design a more anonymous way for people to contribute. This was the best way to overcome the limitations of the strong need to save face.'

There are more tips on virtual working and a link to resources to help you at the book's website: www.facilitatingrisk.com.

MAKE SURE THAT ACTIONS AND DECISIONS ARE CLEARLY AGREED AND DOCUMENTED

This should happen during the session and then be circulated as quickly as possible afterwards. What is going to be done by whom and by when? The right place to document the outputs is almost always the risk register. Unfortunately, this is all too often a dead document, gathering dust, rather than the central repository for all risk based decisions. There is no need for detailed minutes, as these are likely to remain unread. Agree how the actions will be followed up and how will they be reported back to the group.

HOW CAN YOU CHECK WHETHER PEOPLE ARE LIKELY TO DO THEIR ACTIONS?

Ask them about their intentionality – this is the strength of their intent to carry out each action. Penny uses a scale of one to ten and asks people at the end of workshops to report how likely they are to get each action done. If they're unsure that they will be able to do the actions, then she adjusts the action. Surely it is far better to have an imperfect action that's completed, than a perfect one that isn't?

LESSONS LEARNED

While many organisations talk about 'lessons learned', too often these become lessons filed away or even lessons forgotten. What a waste! The risk facilitator can ensure that their risk workshops improve over time by identifying lessons learned with their groups during risk workshops *and* then agreeing actions to take in future workshops as a result. This can be done as simply as taking five minutes each to explore 'what went well' and 'I wish that … .' (Framing things positively is a much more powerful way to learn than 'what went wrong'.)

AFTER THE WORKSHOP

It's very important to share actions and decisions as quickly as possible. Penny likes to take photographs of outputs written up in face-to-face meetings and share them immediately rather than have the details typed up, as these provide a strong visual reminder on top of the formal risk register.

HOW ARE YOU GOING TO FOLLOW UP ON ACTIONS?

Without follow up, actions tend not to happen. Follow up is ideally discussed and agreed at the end of the workshop, before everyone leaves. Ideally, your actions can be added to your project, programme or operations plan immediately after your workshop, as well as to your risk register, so they'll be tracked as part of day-to-day work.

HOW WILL YOU KEEP RISK MANAGEMENT ALIVE FOR THE REST OF THE PROCESS, FOLLOWING THE WORKSHOP?

One way is to ensure that you have identified owners of different risk areas. How will you engage these people going forward? Too many risk identification workshops end up with a completed risk register that is subsequently forgotten about. While this may tick boxes for audit or compliance, it is of no practical use. As the risk facilitator, it's your job to bring energy and life into the process.

You'll need to feed information back to managers in your organisation, your project sponsor and/or the board if appropriate. How will you do this?

SUMMARY

Risk workshops are an inevitable part of the risk management process. Sometimes workshops will take place face-to-face. At other times, the group will be working together from different locations, using tools to support virtual working. It's essential to prepare in advance to ensure you have the best chance of a successful workshop. Facilitating workshops well is an art, and experiencing good risk facilitation is very different from reading it in a book. You will find more helpful hints, tools and templates when you sign up for them at this book's website at www.facilitatingrisk.com, as well as ongoing updates on our work.

In the next chapter, we will run through a range of potential pitfalls for your risk facilitation work, giving you hints and tips to help you avoid them.

REFERENCES

Drexler, A., Sibbet, D. and Forrester, R. (1994) *The Team Performance Model*, San Francisco: The Grove Consultants International.

Tuckmann, B.R. (1965) 'Developmental Sequence in Small Groups'. *Psychological Bulletin*, 63, 384–99.

RECOMMENDED BOOKS

Weisbord, W. and Janoff, S. (2007) *Don't Just Do Something, Stand There: Ten Principles for Leading Meetings That Matter*, San Francisco, CA: Berrett-Koehler Publishers, Inc.

Hunter, D. (2007) *The Art of Facilitation: The Essentials for Leading Great Meetings and Creating Group Synergy*, (2nd edition), Auckland: Random House.

Schwartz, R.M. (2002) *The Skilled Facilitator: A Comprehensive Resource for Consultants, Facilitators, Managers, Trainers, and Coaches*, (2nd edition), San Francisco, CA: Jossey-Bass.

⑥ Potential Pitfalls and How to Overcome Them

This chapter deals with the practical problems and challenges that people face when facilitating risk management: pitfalls that the reader of this book will be able to prepare for and avoid.

Every pitfall described in this chapter has come from a real, current risk practitioner – someone who has shared with us their concerns and frustrations about making risk management work during the year we have been writing this book. Some of the pitfalls are at the heart of risk management, such as people confusing risks with issues. Others are more subtle. We include them all because this chapter is designed to provide immediate help to people who are facilitating risk management work right now.

The chapter is structured into three broad categories:

1. Pitfalls when applying the risk management process.

2. Pitfalls when facilitating.

3. Pitfalls when trying to create a culture where risk management works well.

Each pitfall is stated in capital letters, followed by our response on how best to tackle it. Often, there is more detail elsewhere in the book, but this chapter is meant to give quick, practical advice that the risk facilitator can apply immediately. We suggest that, rather than reading this chapter in detail, you flick through the pitfalls listed below to find those of most relevance to you.

PITFALLS WHEN APPLYING THE RISK MANAGEMENT PROCESS

In this section, you'll find a range of pitfalls related to the process of risk management, along with tips to help you avoid them in the future. We covered the general principles of risk management, along with the outline of a generic process, in Chapters 2 and 4. Some of the guidance will refer you back to those earlier chapters.

WE HAVE NO RISK PROCESS

Chapter 4 gives you the steps in a process and hopefully you can now tailor that to suit your needs. It will be important to agree with the management team how the process will be governed and the roles people will play. Getting as much buy-in to the risk process at the start is vital.

PEOPLE THINK THAT IF WE'VE GOT A RISK REGISTER – HOWEVER PARTIAL – WE ARE DOING RISK MANAGEMENT

It's important to have a risk register, so you have a start, even if your register has cobwebs or is incomplete. The key thing is to improve the content of the risk register and the value that it brings. You could rejuvenate the risk register in a number  of ways, beginning with making sure information from all the steps in the risk management process are included. For example, you could validate the risks on the register with risk owners, refreshing or deleting them as necessary. Alternatively, you could begin the process anew, and tidy the existing risk register as part of a wider risk identification exercise. You can find other ideas in Chapter 4. The key thing is to facilitate some change so that people can start to see the benefits quickly.

THE PEOPLE I WORK WITH DON'T UNDERSTAND THE PROCESS

As risk facilitator, one of your most important roles is to make sure that everyone has a clear understanding about the steps in the risk process and the chance to ask questions if they want to. Often people are confused about what risk management involves and it is important to make sure that questions and misunderstandings are cleared up. Often people will understand the risk management process much better if you explain clearly which part you are focusing on at a particular time. There are different questions to be answered at each step, and different skills involved in doing each step well as outlined in Chapter 4.

MY MANAGER SEEMS TO THINK THAT A COMPLEX PROCESS WILL FIX OUR CURRENT PROBLEMS

It won't. 'Garbage in, garbage out' applies just as much to risk management as to computer systems! The process itself is simple in principle – there's no need to make it more complicated. The difficult part of risk management is engaging the people. That is why facilitation is increasingly recognised as being so crucial.

PEOPLE DON'T UNDERSTAND WHAT RISK IS, OR HAVE UNCLEAR OR EVEN CONFLICTING DEFINITIONS OF RISK

Risks are uncertainties that matter. If something is a fact, it's not uncertain, so it can't be a risk – although it may be the cause of one or more risks. If something is uncertain, but doesn't directly affect the objectives, then it's not a risk to that work – it doesn't matter. It's a good idea to run people through the key concepts around risk, before running a risk workshop or starting the risk management process.

PEOPLE CONFUSE ISSUES WITH RISKS

Issues are known situations that need to be managed. They are not uncertain future events. Issues need to be dealt with, but not by the risk process. Although some people argue that they can effectively manage a process that deals with issue resolution and risk management together, our experience is that this does not work well for either issues or risks. There are links of course. Issues can be causes of risks and unmanaged risks can become issues. We strongly advise you to keep separate logs and have separate discussions of issues and risks in meetings. Otherwise risks (things that might happen) will always take second priority to issues (things actually happening) because they're more urgent, although not necessarily more important.

WHEN I WORK WITH PEOPLE, THEY COME UP WITH 'RISKS'. OFTEN THESE ARE NOT RISK EVENTS, BUT THE CAUSE OR EVEN THE EFFECT OF A RISK. WHAT CAN I DO ABOUT THIS FREQUENT MUDDLE?

It's important to make sure that people understand what a risk event is and how it differs from the cause and the effect. If you don't, then it's almost impossible to prioritise risks and make good decisions about where to focus your time. It can also be really difficult for other people to understand the risk descriptions. Using the three-part risk descriptions works really well. It helps people tease out causes from risk events, and events from effects and brings clarity to the whole process.

Challenge and question people to make sure that your risk register contains risk events, rather than the background cause or the subsequent effect. Re-frame statements that people have made and ask them if this is what they really meant – they are usually grateful for the clarity.

WE TEND TO BE TOO WOOLLY WITH RISKS – WE'RE NOT SPECIFIC ENOUGH. THIS MAKES THEM HARD TO QUANTIFY OR EXPLAIN

Make sure that you've been clear about the big picture and risk categories before moving into the detailed work of identifying risks. Encourage people to be as specific as possible about what might happen and why when they are identifying risks. As risk facilitator, you need to challenge people to provide more detail if required. You may need to help people articulate what the event that may occur actually is, why it may occur and how that would affect the objectives. Try using everyday language, for example: 'what are the things you are worried about?', or 'what are the things that could go better than planned without you doing anything about them?' Then tease out the cause – 'why might that occur?' And the effect – 'what would happen if your worry/hope came true?' Our experience is that people become skilled at this really quickly if you can help them frame their perspective on the risk in question.

ALL THE RISKS WE IDENTIFY ARE OBVIOUS – SO THERE SEEMS THAT NO ADDED VALUE IS GAINED BY GOING THROUGH THE PROCESS

It is a common problem for people to focus mainly on what we'd call 'business-as-usual risks', that is, those things that experience tells you will always be risky in the type of work you do. The normal variability you'd expect in your work, for example based on availability of resources, should be dealt with as part of normal business planning. Risk management is about identifying and managing the 'unusual' risks. As a facilitator, you need to keep the group focused on what's special about the situation in question.

PEOPLE FOCUS ON POTENTIAL THREATS AND TEND TO LEAVE OUT POTENTIAL OPPORTUNITIES

Always start with opportunities. It is very difficult to move into a positive mindset after dealing with threats. If your current process ignores positive opportunities, think about how you can include them. There may not be the same number of good things that might occur as bad ones, but you'll be missing a trick if you don't try. Good things might happen!

DESCRIBING OPPORTUNITIES IS REALLY DIFFICULT – SOMETIMES THEY END UP JUST AS RESPONSES TO THREATS

One of the biggest mistakes people make when starting to work with positive risk is to describe opportunities as binary choices – we could do x, or not. There is no chance of occurrence associated with such a statement – the outcome is in your control: you are either going to do it, or not. The objective in risk management is to focus on *potential* opportunities. These are events that might happen anyway, without any intervention. They are important because they may warrant management effort to make them more likely, or have greater impact. Risk management best practice says that we should, at least, be ready to seize potential opportunities if they occur, because they are rare. So use the format to describe risks that we outlined in Chapter 2 to frame positive risks, and be aware of avoiding descriptions that are just management choices. It takes a bit of practice but works really well once you've mastered the skill.

NO ONE TAKES OWNERSHIP OF RISK

First of all, see if your senior leaders are taking overall ownership of risk management. If leaders are not 'walking the talk', then it can be really difficult to get others to follow. As a facilitator, you can help to coach senior leaders about their role. More practically, you need to make sure that owners are allocated at the risk identification stage. You can also set up follow-up mechanisms for risk owners that make best use of their time. Chapter 4 has some ideas about how to do this. It's really important not to take on the risk ownership role yourself. Stay vegetarian (as described in Chapter 3). You can still offer positive support to the risk owners, without inappropriately taking on their role yourself. Note: the exception to this is if you are performing a dual role, as risk facilitator and a member of the management team for the work. In this situation you may well be a risk owner for some risks, in addition to being the facilitator for others.

PROBABILITY IS HARD TO CALCULATE

Not just hard – impossible in many situations. Unless you have comprehensive historical data that is directly relevant to the risk (which is rare), then all you can do is guess how likely it is that the risk will occur. Start with whether the group judges the risk to be more or less likely to occur, then decide how much more than 50 per cent, or how much less than 50 per cent feels right. Most companies have standard probability scales that force the assessment of probability into a small number of ranges, for example, very high probability is greater than 70 per cent chance. Risk management standards judge this to be best practice.

WE ARE POOR AT PRIORITISATION AND GET BOGGED DOWN AT THIS POINT

People most commonly prioritise risks by using a combination of probability (what's the chance this risk event will happen) and impact (how much it matters if it does). Where risk management standards advise using company standard probability scales as mentioned above, they state that work specific impact scales should be created. Our advice on how to do this is as follows:

- Think about what objectives matter most to your work.

- Define what would be a catastrophic impact on each objective, for example, what time delay would be a 'show-stopper'.

- Define what impact would be insignificant, for example, the amount of money that it is not worth proactively trying to save.

- Define impact scales (three, four, or five categories) that represent the specific impact on objectives that would really matter to your work.

- If you invest time in doing this, that is, defining how you will prioritise before you start, it will save you hours of frustration later.

WE DO A REASONABLE JOB AT PRIORITISATION, BUT THEN IGNORE LOW PRIORITY RISKS

As we have pointed out in Chapter 5, it is really important that the facilitator helps the group focus on the highest priority risks at each workshop. But the risk prioritisation is only a snapshot in time. Who's to say that the assessment of probability and impact will be the same in a month's time? The risk owner is the person who should keep an eye on this, but as facilitator you may need to play an active role to ensure this happens. It might be necessary at some point to hold a special session to readdress those lower priority risks and see what can be learned.

WE NEED TO USE APPROPRIATE WAYS TO RESPOND TO RISK – NOT JUST MITIGATE!

There are many different ways to respond to risks. The option you choose will depend on a number of things, including the appetite for risk (how much uncertainty can you tolerate?) and the resources available (does it make sense to invest time and money now to reduce the uncertainty?). Chapter 2 has a whole section on responding to risks, outlining all the options you can choose. Why not use the guidance in the response planning section of Chapter 4 with your group and overtly consider options other than mitigation, which is only relevant to reducing a bad risk. Changing language often leads to a change in thinking, that is very beneficial for the overall process.

OUT OF THE FRYING PAN, INTO THE FIRE: WE ALWAYS SEEM TO FORGET ABOUT THE SECONDARY RISK

Identification of secondary risks is a part of response planning. Make sure your process makes this crystal clear and that risk owners understand their responsibilities. A response plan is not complete without secondary risks identified and described well in the risk register. We find also that when you make this a discipline, you get a much better quality of risk response in the first place, because all the consequences are thought through.

PEOPLE TEND NOT TO FOLLOW UP ON THE RISK PLAN

Why have a separate risk plan, if actions don't happen? Add the risk actions into the project, programme or operational plan so you can be sure they are resourced and monitored. You also need to find ways of holding risk owners accountable. There are ideas to help you in Chapter 4.

WE OFTEN LEAVE WORKSHOPS WITH POOR OUTCOMES: INAPPROPRIATE ACTIONS OR NO AGREED PLAN TO MANAGE, OR BOTH

Come to an agreement about outcomes of your workshop at the start, using the start-up process outlined in Chapter 5. Challenge actions if you feel they are inappropriate. It is also important to check people's intent to carry out their specific risk response actions. Put in place some sort of follow-up mechanism.

WE LEAVE WORKSHOPS WITH PLANS, THEN BEHAVE AS IF THE RISK HAS ALREADY BEEN MANAGED

A few months ago Ruth was speaking with a colleague, who is a very experienced risk consultant. During the conversation, it became apparent that even experienced people can be fooled into thinking that a plan to respond to a risk is a 'done deal'. Of course, a plan to respond is just that. It needs to be resourced and implemented if the exposure to risk is to be changed. The example we were discussing involved eliminating the cause of a threat. It would be normal to say the residual risk was zero in this situation, but of course this is only true *if* the response plan has been successfully implemented. Facilitators need to be very clear with their language, and talk about the risk remaining should the plan be unsuccessful. We also need good systems for tracking and monitoring the success of response actions. If we leave out this step, we are only doing risk assessment, not managing risks properly.

WE HANDLE RISKS BY LISTING PROBLEMS AND, ALL TOO OFTEN, RANDOM THOUGHTS

By raising this as a problem, you know that this isn't too useful. Look at Chapter 4 to gain a fuller understanding of the steps you need to cover along with the process that you can follow and adapt to suit your organisation. But don't lose those inputs, just turn them into good risk descriptions later. People are likely to be grateful that their thoughts have been listened to and channelled into a useful process.

I'M A BUSINESS ANALYST, WORKING WITH REQUIREMENTS. WE DON'T HAVE ANY TRACEABILITY OF RISKS TO REQUIREMENTS. THIS CAN CAUSE PROBLEMS WITH CHANGES OF SCOPE

Add in traceability if that will help your work. When considering risks to requirements, you could hold a separate workshop. During this workshop you could link each risk to the appropriate requirement.

PITFALLS WHEN FACILITATING

You can find advice about facilitation, both in and out of workshops in Chapters 3 and 5. In this section, you'll find some quick tips about avoiding pitfalls in future when you are facilitating.

I DON'T KNOW HOW IT HAPPENS, BUT WHENEVER I WORK WITH GROUPS I ALWAYS SEEM TO END UP WITH THE ACTIONS. WHAT CAN I DO?

This is fundamental to risk facilitation. Risks are uncertainties that matter to the group's objectives, not yours. This is something you need to reflect throughout the risk process. Remind the group that you are there to make their process easy, but that they own the risks. There are lots of tips on how to do this in Chapters 3, 4 and 5.

TOO OFTEN, WE 'DO' RISK AT THE START, THEN 'IT'S DONE' SO WE LEAVE IT ALONE AND THE PROCESS DIES

Don't worry, you are not alone! Avoiding this is the main point of risk facilitation. We've found many organisations where risk is 'done' at the start for compliance reasons and then abandoned once the boxes are ticked. This is a waste of time and money. Having said that, can you adapt the tick boxes into action steps and use these with other tools to form part of your risk process?

We recommend that you develop your skills as a risk facilitator, particularly focusing on engaging people and energising the risk process to keep it alive.

MY ORGANISATION HAS NO CONCEPT OF A RISK FACILITATOR

Risk facilitation is a new skill that is becoming more important as organisations take on increasing amounts of change and more risky new ventures. Even facilitation is a fairly new profession that is developing rapidly, as is risk management. By combining the two, you're becoming a pioneer, likely to add much value over the years ahead.

Remember too that to become a really effective risk facilitator, you will need to change the culture of your organisation, particularly their attitude towards risk management.

See Vivien and Anna's stories in Chapter 3 for inspiration on how to turn this from 'boring and necessary' to 'beneficial and essential'.

SOME OF OUR RISK FACILITATORS GET FAR TOO INVOLVED

It is quite common for the manager to attempt to be the risk facilitator for their own work. The trouble here is that the manager is then tied up facilitating the workshop, rather than giving their unique view on the risks. Worse still, in this situation the facilitator may only give air-time to views that support their own. We recommend the use of an independent facilitator. This person could be another manager on an exchange from another part of the organisation, for example a project management office, or could be an external consultant. Remember that they need to understand both risk, and facilitation as well as being experienced in running risk workshops (see the hamburger model – with the lettuce and tomato in Chapter 3).

WE HAVE PEOPLE WHO ARE MEANT TO MANAGE RISK, BUT THEY ARE INCOMPETENT AS FACILITATORS

This book has explained why facilitation is essential to making risk management work. Can these risk managers become good facilitators with support and training? If not, you may need to change the way your organisation manages risk or bring in new people with the appropriate skills in both risk *and* facilitation.

I HAVE BEEN DOING RISK FACILITATION FOR YEARS, SOMETIMES MAKING IT UP AS I GO ALONG. HOW CAN I TAKE WHAT I'VE LEARNT FROM THIS BOOK AND DEVELOP MY SKILLS FURTHER, AS WELL AS ADDING SOME THEORETICAL UNDERPINNING OF WHAT I ALREADY KNOW?

As we've said before, facilitation is a fairly new skill and its application to risk management is even newer. Congratulations for developing your skills and competence through years of practice and learning lessons as you go.

To develop a theoretical underpinning of what you already know, and build on the contents of this book, you could join a risk facilitation course. Look for ones that combine expertise in risk and facilitation, enabling you to learn from both disciplines at the same time. The alternative is to join a general facilitation course, although this will not cover the subtle and specialist areas of risk management. For more information, see www.facilitatingrisk.com.

PEOPLE DON'T UNDERSTAND THE POINT OF THE WORKSHOP

This is fundamental. Everything else flows from this. You need to be really clear about the purpose of the workshop, both in the preparation phase, and at the start of the actual session. Successful workshops can flow from an agreed purpose. Confusion about the purpose almost always results in poor outcomes.

WE TEND TO LACK CLEAR OBJECTIVES WHEN I ATTEND RISK WORKSHOPS

The facilitator needs to set up and agree clear objectives as well as the time plan, roles, ground rules and what happens next at the start of each meeting.

POOR FACILITATION HINDERS OUR WORKSHOPS

It happens! You can learn facilitation from risk facilitation experts or alternatively bring in experienced facilitators to run some of your risk workshops. Watching experienced facilitators is one way that people learn that good facilitation is crucial to making the risk management process work.

WE USUALLY HAVE THE WRONG PEOPLE IN THE WORKSHOP. EITHER SOME ARE MISSING OR TOO MANY ATTEND. OFTEN IT'S HARD TO GET THE RIGHT PEOPLE TO TURN UP

People are much more likely to attend if they know the session will be interesting and worthwhile. As previously mentioned, it's important to be really clear about the point of your risk workshop, in particular which steps of the risk management process you plan to address. If you do this it should be easier to work out who needs to be there and who doesn't. It's much easier to convince people that they are needed (or not!) if you have a clear purpose and objectives for each workshop.

In order to get the right people to attend, you need to convince them of the benefits of the workshop and why they need to be there. This may require one-to-one conversations with key people prior to your workshop to convince them.

Another way to make it more likely that people will attend is to ask for their input about which date suits them best. If you've done this, it is harder for them to refuse to come if you hold the workshop on a date they've already agreed with.

Once you have people in the room, you can engage their interest and enthusiasm by running a very effective and enjoyable workshop using the tips in Chapter 5. Risk workshops have all too often been seen as boring and, once this belief is shattered, you should find it less of a challenge to get people to attend.

IN OUR WORKSHOPS THE ORGANISATIONAL CULTURE AND POLITICS ARE OFTEN NOT UNDERSTOOD AND THIS CAUSES PROBLEMS

It is normal for workshops to bring people together from different parts of an organisation. Not only that, but sometimes there will be people from other organisations present, for example a client, key supplier, partner or regulator. It is therefore quite normal for people to have different goals, styles and ways of working. The more you prepare in advance the better. Try to find out as much as you can about the workshop participants, so you can plan your approach accordingly. The more you, as facilitator, understand about organisational culture, the more you can anticipate and respond to problems if they arise. You are ideally placed to treat everyone with equal respect. When you do this, you may well find that everyone else follows your example. Your role is to make sure everyone can contribute despite the organisational culture and politics.

IT SEEMS THAT WE ARE TOO CLOSE TO THE DETAIL WHEN WE COME UP WITH RISKS; WE DON'T HAVE A HOLISTIC VIEW

There are a few ways that facilitators can help here. One is by focusing the team on what matters, that is, the objectives. While some of these will be detailed, there will be other, more holistic objectives, that need attention too. Another way that a facilitator can help is by using prompt lists to help people think across all areas. A generic example would be to use the PESTLE prompt (Political, Economical, Sociological, Technological, Legal, Environmental). There are many other ways to structure prompt lists to help the team think broadly, as well as deeply.

WE TEND TO GO OFF TRACK AND LOSE FOCUS

Keep the purpose of your workshop at the front of everybody's mind by writing it up on the wall or placing it in a shared area of your screen. It is the facilitator's main role to keep people 'on purpose' and to flag up when the group drifts off track. One way of doing this in a face-to-face meeting is to give each person two cards – one red and the other one yellow. Using a football referee analogy, explain at the start of the meeting that they can wave a yellow card if the meeting starts to go off track. This is usually enough to bring people back to the point with a smile! Using this method our experience is that red cards, signifying a major issue, are seldom required.

WE GET OVERWHELMED BY DETAIL

There can be a lot of detail in a risk workshop. Make sure the big picture and benefits are visible to all throughout the workshop. Also keep to an appropriate level of detail for the audience. You may also find that you are simply trying to do too much in one workshop. Chapter 4 provides some tips about splitting up the risk process and using a combination of workshops, and work outside of such sessions.

WE CAN'T SEEM TO IDENTIFY RISKS

Risks aren't always easy to find, are they? Go through the process outlined in Chapter 4. Start with causes – things happening now – that can stimulate thought. Make sure that you have a wide range of people involved so that all areas are covered. Use creativity to help people to come up with a range of ideas.

WHY DO I NEED TO CARE ABOUT RISK ATTITUDE?

In short, risk attitude is important because ignoring it will mean that human perspectives are unmanaged, potentially leading to bias and poor-quality decision-making. Risk attitude is used to describe a person's chosen response to a risk. Risk attitude is personal, situational and driven by perceptions. This means that your risk attitudes vary from time to time. Groups can also hold risk attitudes. Again, you should expect these also to vary from time to time, depending on the situational and other factors that influence perception (see Chapter 2, Appendix A).

Risk attitude is normally expressed by using labels such as:

- *Risk averse* meaning that the person would choose to act in order to increase certainty.

- *Risk seeking* meaning that the person would be comfortable with the uncertainty without doing anything to reduce it.

Other labels commonly used are risk tolerant and risk neutral – see Chapter 2 for more details. Risk attitude is a massive subject, although you can gain a good grasp fairly quickly if you want to. A good place to start is www.risk-attitude.com.

PEOPLE I WORK WITH ARE VERY RISK AVERSE

We need to be careful about labelling whole groups of people in this way. It may well be that the prevailing culture of your organisation is to minimise uncertainty as far as possible and to feel uncomfortable if there are unmanaged risks about – that's what risk averse means – but that doesn't mean that it's useful to assume that all people will always behave like that. In a typical working team there will be a whole range of risk attitudes 'in the room'. A crucial skill of the facilitator is to be aware of your own attitude to risk at that time, and to be able to spot decision-biases that may be arising from inappropriate risk attitudes. Sometimes it's good just to name what you see, bring the risk attitude or bias to the attention of the group so you can help them explore what's going on. It also helps to be clear about risk appetite and what tolerance for risk the organisation has – see Chapter 2 for more on this.

TOO OFTEN, WE HAVE POWERFUL PEOPLE IN THE ROOM AND THEY TEND TO SWAY OR BLOCK RISKS. SENIOR PEOPLE INFLUENCE OR SOMETIMES EVEN DIRECT DISCUSSION. HOW CAN WE DEAL WITH THIS?

Make sure that you are aware of any senior (or very junior) people who might cause hierarchy to be an issue within your workshop. You might need to plan a range of processes to keep the workshop on track. In some circumstances, it makes sense to discuss this issue with the attendees individually, explaining that in order to assess risks properly, everyone's input is needed. It can be useful to design the process for anonymous input (either before or during the workshop), or splitting into small groups and then presenting back as a group, rather than individually.

SOME PEOPLE ARE NATURALLY DOMINANT AND TALK OVER OTHERS

Yes, they are. If you have someone who is speaking much more than everyone else, it will affect your workshop. Find out if this is likely, given past experiences. During the workshop, there are several ways to deal with this. The easiest is calling a break and talking to the individual concerned. Often, just pointing out to the group as a whole that one person has been speaking for ten minutes and asking what they'd like to do about this, can do the trick. It may be that they are happy to hear more from him or her. This solution also has the added bonus of leaving the ownership of the problem with the group, rather than trying to solve it yourself.

KEY PEOPLE KEEP QUIET IN MY WORKSHOPS

Prepare beforehand for the range of people who will be in your workshop. If you know that some people are unlikely to speak up, then you can plan different ways to obtain their input. As with the previous pitfall, anonymous input can be useful, such as writing on sticky notes, or breaking into small groups for discussion and then reporting back. If your quiet people are happy to speak out to the whole group as long as they are not interrupted, then you could use the 'talking stick' approach. In this approach you choose an object to act as a 'talking stick' and set a rule that the only person allowed to speak is the one holding the stick.

GROUPS I LEAD OFTEN SPEND TOO LONG CONCENTRATING ON THE 'WRONG' RISKS, FOR EXAMPLE THOSE WITH LOW PROBABILITY AND LOW IMPACT

It's true that low probability, low impact risks are not the top priority – but that doesn't mean they can be ignored. Each one of those will have a risk owner who is hopefully keeping an eye on the risky situation. Nevertheless, your job as a risk facilitator is to help the group use their time to best effect, so you can challenge people if they are clearly not focusing on the priority matters. Remember also what we've said in Chapter 4 about not doing everything in workshops. Risk response planning is something that can be done by the risk owner once all the risks to objectives have been identified and prioritised.

I DON'T GET HONEST ANSWERS WHEN I ASK PEOPLE ABOUT RISKS

That's interesting. What do you mean by an honest answer? It sounds as if there is some background work for you to do as a facilitator before your workshops and to talk with the individuals involved. Is it just a different viewpoint? What are the political issues involved?

WHAT ABOUT VESTED INTERESTS?

We all have vested interests. People in your workshops will come from a variety of areas and of course they will have their own interests at heart. It is your job as a facilitator to help the group to find a way of working through any challenges.

PEOPLE KEEP INVENTING INAPPLICABLE OR UNREALISTIC RISKS

If you are using techniques such as brainstorming, then it is natural that some inapplicable risks will be raised because we want people to open up and be creative. At this stage, quantity is more important than quality. But quality needs to follow as the initial brainstorm is turned into well-described risks. Only at this consolidation point should points be removed, if they are not uncertainties that would matter if they occurred. Of course, it really helps if you are very clear about the objectives and impact areas that matter the most before starting to identify risks. It can also help to use risk categories to achieve this same purpose.

WE NEED MORE THAN ONE WORKSHOP BUT IT IS SO HARD TO ENGAGE PEOPLE AND RETAIN THEIR COMMITMENT. WHAT SHOULD WE DO?

It is usual to need more than one workshop. In fact we would strongly urge that risk management work takes place over a series of activities, only some of which are workshops. Resist the pressure to cram all of the risk work into one marathon session. Your challenge is to engage people. A series of much shorter, but effective, risk workshops might well do the trick, especially if they are tightly focused and fun to participate in.

IT'S A CHALLENGE TO MAINTAIN REGULAR ATTENDANCE AT RISK WORKSHOPS

We'd suggest that the first step is to make sure that you really need the same people at each session. Do these sessions have a clear reason to exist other than the fact that it is a particular time of the month? You may well find that each workshop needs a slightly different set of participants. If the same people are needed each time, perhaps you could vary the format of the workshop, trying new techniques to achieve the same objectives. If you can keep the sessions interesting, people are more likely to make them a priority. Of course, there may be times when people want to attend, but cannot. Then you need to think about how you can include them virtually in some way.

WE CAN'T MEET FACE-TO-FACE TO RUN A RISK WORKSHOP AS WE'RE SPREAD OUT GEOGRAPHICALLY

Run your workshop virtually using audio conferencing and shared screens. Virtual workshops need experienced facilitators.

If you're not used to working in this way, consider bringing in an external facilitator. You'll need to make sure that they have experience with facilitating risk *and* working virtually. Good virtual workshops are not just about having access to the right technology, although this helps enormously.

I'M TERRIFIED OF DESTRUCTIVE CONFRONTATION AT MY WORKSHOP

If you think this is likely you need to take even more care to follow good practice. Set up ground rules in advance, before confrontation happens. Facilitate any conflict carefully. Always remain open to task conflict, that is, where people have different viewpoints based on their role and experience. Make sure everyone who needs to has an opportunity to have their say. This is necessary for good decision-making.

Relationship conflict is another matter. Address this as soon as you can, as it can be very destructive. There are ideas on how to do this in Chapter 5.

OUR WORKSHOPS CONTAIN SO MANY DIFFERENT CULTURAL PERSPECTIVES, TOLERANCES, AND ATTITUDES TO RISK. HOW CAN WE COPE?

First of all, by acknowledging that this is normal. As part of your stakeholder analysis, you need to find out as much as possible about the participants who will attend. This will help you plan sessions that respect cultural differences and get the best out of people. Of course you will learn a lot more within a session if you are able to remain 'present' and open to the people. There are some helpful hints how to do this in Chapter 5.

SOMETIMES PEOPLE IN WORKSHOPS SEEM TO FEAR IDENTIFYING RISKS, AS IF BY MENTIONING THEM, THEY'RE MAKING THE RISK MORE LIKELY – WHY?

Although it may sound silly to suggest that simply mentioning a risk might 'tempt fate' and make it more likely, we know people have this view. The reality is that the reverse happens. Articulating a risk opens up our senses to think what we might do about it. We can't actively respond to every risk, but we can be mindful, with our 'radar' tuned in. Facilitators should put effort into ensuring they create as safe a place as possible for risk identification so that the process is as creative and divergent as you can make it. The risks that individuals think about but don't share, may well be the be the very ones that actually occur.

PEOPLE USE JARGON OR TECHNICAL LANGUAGE THAT HALF THE GROUP DON'T UNDERSTAND

As facilitator, you will need to make sure that any jargon or technical language is translated so that everyone can understand. People don't like to own up to not understanding jargon though, so you will need to ask simple questions such as 'What do you mean by that three letter abbreviation?' You'll find that many others in your workshop will be thinking the same, but are reluctant to ask such 'dumb questions'. In reality, these are intelligent questions that need asking. As facilitator, you need to be brave. Others will respect you for making things clear.

WE ALWAYS SEEM TO RUN OUT OF TIME

This is a perennial problem, with poor facilitation at the root. Be clear from the start what your purpose and objectives are for a session. Arrange multiple, shorter workshops rather than trying to get everything done in one go. Design a clear time plan with realistic amounts of time for each part. An experienced facilitator can help here, even if they're only available in the design phase. Appoint a timekeeper.

WE DON'T HAVE ENOUGH TIME TO REACH A CONSENSUS

Is true consensus really necessary for your group? If so, you need to plan in enough time to get there. If not, stop once you have what you need.

WHAT RISK WORKSHOP? IN OUR ORGANISATION, RISK WORKSHOPS ARE NOT AN ACCEPTED WAY OF DEALING WITH RISK AS YOU'RE EXPECTED TO WORK ON THIS ALONE

Explain that effective risk management relies on having a variety of different perspectives from stakeholders to gain a full picture of the risks that are perceived to exist. By working on risk management on your own, you're likely to miss out many important risks. Another benefit of workshops is that a great deal of information can be analysed by the group in a much shorter time than if you were to go and talk to each stakeholder in turn. You can gain instant feedback too. Having said all that, it is important to remember that not all the steps in the risk management process are best suited to workshops (see Chapter 4).

PEOPLE DON'T UNDERSTAND WHY WE NEED A WORKSHOP AT ALL

Explain the purpose of the workshop before convening the group (either face-to-face or virtually). Make sure that the people involved understand what each session needs to achieve and what their role in the workshop will be. Add in the benefits of risk workshops and how much value they can add.

OUR WORKSHOPS ARE NOT TAILORED CORRECTLY

Well, now's a good time to get going. As a risk facilitator, you need to adapt to suit the different cultures (profession, countries and organisations) involved.

IN OUR ORGANISATION, RISKS ARE NOT PUBLISHED AND SHARED. THERE IS A LOT OF SECRECY INVOLVED

Is there a good reason for the secrecy? Challenge this if not. You may need to adapt the workshop to allow for the right levels of confidentiality.

OUR WORKSHOPS ARE SCUPPERED BY HIDDEN AGENDAS AND POLITICS

Prepare well and ask stakeholders about the possible impact of politics and hidden agendas beforehand. Set up and agree ground rules. If you assume good intent from everyone, you'll be more likely to get it. If you wouldn't describe yourself as politically savvy, make sure that there are others in the room who are able to help you to be effective, despite politics. Ensure you have a senior sponsor to start off your workshop and, if appropriate, to remain throughout.

RISK WORKSHOPS ARE BORING AND SEEN AS UNCREATIVE

We've shared lots of ideas to overcome this throughout this book. We encourage you to try some of them and to let us know how you get along. There is lots of additional help that can be provided once you have some experience of the fundamentals we have explained.

PITFALLS WHEN TRYING TO CREATE A CULTURE WHERE RISK MANAGEMENT WORKS WELL

REACTIVE HEROES, NOT PROACTIVE RISK MANAGERS, ARE VALUED IN MY ORGANISATION

We often hear people say this. Fortunately we hear this from senior leaders as much as from their  staff and this is positive as we detect a real desire to change. Leaders, at all levels, have to take responsibility for making the change. It can really help to set personal objectives for all staff that encourage proactive and anticipatory behaviours. Our experience is that the culture starts to change when money spent on actual problems (issues) is tracked, *and* there is a focus on learning lessons from completed work. Most importantly, everyone needs to 'walk the talk', that is, make it a daily habit to discuss what's risky and why.

WE'RE SO BUSY DOING DAY-TO-DAY DELIVERY THAT RISK MANAGEMENT GETS SQUEEZED OUT

Yes, but how much of your day-to-day delivery is caused by managing actual problems and fire-fighting? Many of your current issues would once have been uncertain threats, which could have been managed proactively. What about your missed opportunities? Until you put an appropriate risk management process into place, you'll continue to be affected by avoidable issues and missed opportunities. Unfortunately, to see an improvement, you need to put in additional effort in the short term. This quickly repays as you start to manage risks and so there are fewer crises.

NO ONE CAN SEE THE PAIN WE'RE AVOIDING. WE'RE NOT NOTICING THE IMPROVEMENTS WE MAKE

This is a tricky one. Of course the work that you do to avoid costly threats is valuable. But to convince others of the value of your work, you will need to measure it in some way. See Chapter 2 for ideas on what to measure.

SENIOR MANAGERS IN MY ORGANISATION DON'T BUY IN TO RISK. THEY CAN'T SEE THE VALUE. IT'S SEEN AS A WASTE OF TIME AND COUNTERPRODUCTIVE

This is another area where measures can help. The base-line metrics of 'how it is now' can be an eye-opener for senior managers who may not have paid much attention to the detail of risk management. To build support, you need to be able to explain – or better still – show the benefits of risk management to people in your organisation at all levels. See Vivien's story and Anna's story in Chapter 3 to see how they were influential in their respective organisations. This may involve learning lessons from past failures in managing risk. Offering appropriate training can help spread the understanding across your organisation. The key thing though is to focus on what matters most, and make progress visible.

MY ORGANISATION TENDS TO 'JUMP ON' ANYONE WHO COMES UP WITH NEGATIVE THREATS. HOW CAN I BRING IN GOOD RISK MANAGEMENT PRACTICES WITHOUT LIMITING MY CAREER?

The most effective environment for risk management is one where there is a 'no-blame' culture. In such a culture, people are rewarded for highlighting threats that can then dealt with appropriately in advance of any negative impact. Think about how you can encourage this. Sometimes it's useful to talk about a possible response to a threat when you first mention it. Doing this is often perceived as positive, that is 'this bad thing may happen, but we can do this now ...'. Raising the risk only, with no potential solution, can be seen as negative. In our experience though, negative reactions to risk identification from senior management can often happen when risk registers are full of 'normal' risk, such as statements like 'we may not have the resources when we need them'. This is not useful. General variability about resource availability needs to be built into plans. Specific risks associated with specific resources for specific work are useful to include in the risk register only if the resource type is scarce and the work is critical.

WHEN WE PRESENT THE RESULTS OF OUR WORKSHOPS, SENIOR MANAGERS THINK WE'RE BEING NEGATIVE. THEY SAY THINGS LIKE: 'I WANT A CAN-DO ATTITUDE – SOLUTIONS NOT PROBLEMS'

It's important to make sure that the senior managers understand the benefits of good risk management. Once that's in place, then make sure you present both positive opportunities as well as the negative threats. Be careful to present these at an appropriate level of detail for the people you're presenting to. With senior managers, this can be much more 'big picture' than the risk facilitator is used to.

OUR ORGANISATION LACKS DEEP EXPERIENCE IN RISK AND IN RISK FACILITATION. HOW CAN WE DEVELOP THIS QUICKLY?

While this book has a detailed plan for doing risk management it can take some time to build up from scratch. This can be speeded up by bringing in risk facilitation experts to support you whilst your organisation is developing. With help, people can develop the skills they need for your organisation to become self-sufficient in implementing effective risk management.

This chapter has discussed many pitfalls, all raised by existing risk practitioners. You may be feeling a little overwhelmed with all the detail. We'll therefore finish this book with a quick summary – our Ten Golden Guidelines for the Risk Facilitator.

7 Ten Golden Guidelines for the Risk Facilitator

This final chapter is deliberately very short. It summarises the book with ten golden guidelines for anyone involved in facilitating risk management.

1. There are lots of pitfalls, but you can plan and prepare carefully and avoid falling into them.

2. Risk management is difficult to do well, and a facilitator can make a big difference. The role of the facilitator is to make it easy.

3. Risk facilitators need a whole range of personal qualities, as well as a deep understanding of the risk management process.

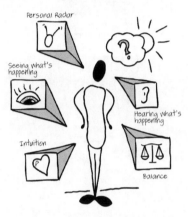

4. Risk facilitators also need to be 'vegetarian'. They focus on the facilitation process, and the risk management process, but stay out of the 'meat' of the work content.

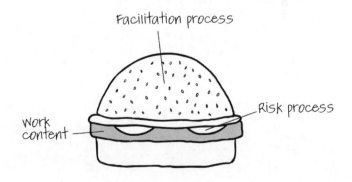

5. Risk facilitators need to engage the right people at all times.

6. Risk facilitators need to keep groups energised, as well as engaged, while maintaining their own level of energy.

7. Risk facilitators add lots of value when they have the skills and credibility to challenge the participants. They need to resist the temptation to challenge on content, staying vegetarian.

8. Careful preparation is the key to successful workshops.

9. Things do go wrong. Different people have different perceptions of what is risky and why. Conflicts will arise. Stay calm and help the group to find a way through.

10. Facilitate risk management well, and you'll engage others and make sure that the risk register is cobweb-free!

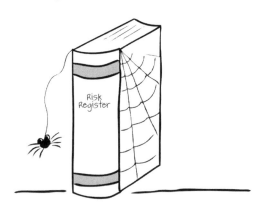

Risk management is very important if organisations are to make good decisions in risky and important situations. As a risk facilitator, you can add real value by making the process easy for your colleagues, so they can be creative, productive and have fun.

Index